All About Arctic Circle: A Kid's Guide to Life at the Top of the World

Educational Books For Kids, Volume 14

Shah Rukh

Published by Shah Rukh, 2024.

While every precaution has been taken in the preparation of this book, the publisher assumes no responsibility for errors or omissions, or for damages resulting from the use of the information contained herein.

ALL ABOUT ARCTIC CIRCLE: A KID'S GUIDE TO LIFE AT THE TOP OF THE WORLD

First edition. September 22, 2024.

ISBN: 979-8227179593

Written by Shah Rukh.

Table of Contents

Prologue

Welcome to the Arctic Circle, a magical land at the very top of our planet! Here, the sun shines brightly in the summer, creating a never-ending day, while in winter, the night stretches on with stunning displays of the Northern Lights. This extraordinary place is home to incredible animals, vibrant cultures, and breathtaking landscapes that seem to belong to another world.

In this guide, we will embark on an exciting journey through the Arctic Circle. You'll meet the majestic polar bears, discover how the Inuit people have thrived in this harsh environment, and learn about the mysterious secrets hidden beneath the icy waters. You'll see how the Arctic is changing and what we can do to help protect it.

Whether you dream of exploring the frozen tundra, witnessing the beauty of the auroras, or understanding the delicate balance of life in this extreme habitat, this book is your gateway to adventure. So, bundle up, open your mind, and get ready to dive into the wonders of the Arctic Circle!

Chapter 1: Polar Bears of the Arctic

Polar bears are one of the most iconic and majestic animals of the Arctic. These magnificent creatures are uniquely adapted to survive in one of the harshest environments on Earth, and they hold a special place in the ecosystem of the Arctic Circle. To truly understand the life of a polar bear, we must explore not only their physical characteristics but also their behavior, diet, hunting techniques, and the challenges they face due to the changing climate.

Polar bears are the largest land carnivores, with adult males, also known as boars, weighing between 900 and 1,600 pounds, and measuring around 8 to 10 feet long from nose to tail. Females, or sows, are smaller, typically weighing between 400 and 700 pounds. Despite their massive size, polar bears are incredibly agile and powerful swimmers, often traveling great distances across the Arctic Ocean in search of food and ice. Their bodies are built for the cold; they have a thick layer of blubber beneath their skin that provides insulation, along with two layers of fur that help trap heat. The outer layer of their fur is oily and water-repellent, which helps them stay dry after swimming in the freezing waters. Interestingly, although polar bears appear white, their fur is actually translucent, and their skin underneath is black, which helps absorb heat from the sun.

The primary habitat of polar bears is on the sea ice that forms over the Arctic Ocean. They spend much of their time on the ice hunting for seals, which make up the bulk of their diet. Seals, particularly ringed and bearded seals, are abundant in the Arctic and are rich in fat, which is essential for polar bears to maintain their energy reserves. Polar bears are highly specialized hunters, and their hunting strategy involves a method known as "still-hunting." They wait patiently by a seal's breathing hole in the ice, sometimes for hours or even days, until a seal surfaces to breathe. When the seal comes up for air, the polar bear strikes with lightning speed, using its powerful paws and sharp claws to grab the seal and drag it onto the ice.

Another hunting technique polar bears use is stalking seals that are resting on the ice. They approach their prey stealthily, often blending in with the snowy environment, and once within range, they charge at the seal with incredible speed, despite their large size. In addition to seals, polar bears may occasionally hunt other animals, such as walruses or beluga whales, although these preys are much more difficult to catch. Polar bears are also known to scavenge on the remains of whale carcasses that wash ashore, providing them with a much-needed meal, especially during the summer months when the sea ice is sparse.

Polar bears are solitary animals, except for mothers with cubs or during the breeding season. Mating takes place in the spring, and after a gestation period of about eight months, females give birth to one to three cubs in the winter. Polar bear mothers are extremely protective of their young and will nurse them in dens made of snow and ice for several months. The cubs are born blind and helpless, weighing only about one pound at birth, but they grow rapidly under the care of their mother, feeding on her rich milk, which is about 30% fat. The mother polar bear stays with her cubs for about two to three years, teaching them how to hunt and survive in the Arctic environment.

The Arctic is a harsh and unforgiving place, and polar bears must contend with extreme cold, long periods of darkness during the polar winter, and the constant challenge of finding enough food to sustain themselves. Their reliance on sea ice for hunting makes them especially vulnerable to the effects of climate change. As the Earth's temperature rises, the Arctic sea ice is melting at an alarming rate, reducing the polar bear's hunting grounds. In some areas, polar bears are forced to travel greater distances to find ice, expending more energy than they can replenish from their food sources. This has led to an increase in polar bear-human interactions, as hungry bears are driven closer to coastal communities in search of food.

In addition to the threat posed by climate change, polar bears also face challenges from pollution. Industrial pollutants such as heavy metals and chemicals can accumulate in the Arctic through ocean currents and atmospheric circulation. These pollutants can build up in the food chain, eventually reaching polar bears through the seals they eat. Some studies have shown that these pollutants can affect polar bears' reproductive health and immune systems, making it harder for them to survive in an already difficult environment.

Polar bears have long held cultural significance for the Indigenous peoples of the Arctic, such as the Inuit, who have lived alongside these animals for thousands of years. In many Indigenous cultures, polar bears are revered as powerful spiritual beings and are often featured in stories and legends. The Inuit, for example, have great respect for the polar bear's strength, endurance, and ability to survive in the cold. Historically, polar bears have also been an important source of food and materials for Arctic communities. Indigenous hunters used every part of the polar bear, from its fur for clothing to its meat for sustenance, in a way that ensured the survival of both people and the animal populations.

Polar bears have become a symbol of the Arctic's pristine wilderness, but they are also a stark reminder of the impact human activities are having on the environment. Conservation efforts are underway to protect polar bears and their habitat, but the challenges are immense. International agreements, such as the Agreement on the Conservation of Polar Bears, signed in 1973, aim to regulate polar bear hunting and promote research on the species. In some areas, polar bears are listed as threatened or endangered, depending on the severity of the threats they face in specific regions.

Despite these efforts, the future of polar bears remains uncertain. Scientists predict that if current trends in global warming continue, the Arctic could be largely ice-free during the summer months within the next few decades. Without sea ice, polar bears will lose their primary hunting grounds, leading to further declines in their population. Some polar bears may adapt to living on land and scavenging for food, but this will likely not be enough to sustain them in the long term.

Polar bears are not only a vital part of the Arctic ecosystem but also a powerful symbol of the natural world's fragility. Their future depends on the actions we take to address climate change and protect the Arctic environment. Educating people, especially younger generations, about the importance of polar bears and their role in the Arctic ecosystem is crucial in the fight to save them. Polar bears teach us about resilience, survival, and the delicate balance of nature, and their plight should inspire us to take meaningful action to preserve the Arctic for future generations.

In conclusion, polar bears are extraordinary animals with remarkable adaptations that allow them to thrive in the harsh Arctic environment. They are skilled hunters, devoted mothers, and an integral part of the Arctic food chain. However, the challenges they face from climate change, pollution, and habitat loss are significant, and their survival is increasingly at risk. Protecting polar bears and the Arctic ecosystem requires global cooperation and a commitment to reducing the impact of human activities on the environment. If we can take the necessary steps to address these issues, we may be able to secure a future for these majestic creatures and the fragile world they inhabit.

Chapter 2: The Northern Lights Magic

The Northern Lights, or Aurora Borealis, is one of the most magical and awe-inspiring natural phenomena that occur in the Arctic Circle and other regions near the Earth's magnetic poles. This dazzling display of colorful lights dancing across the night sky has captivated people for centuries, inspiring countless legends, scientific studies, and deep wonder about the workings of our planet and the universe. While the scientific explanation behind the Northern Lights is fascinating, the emotional impact of witnessing them firsthand is truly extraordinary. To fully appreciate the magic of the Northern Lights, it's important to explore their origins, how they form, their cultural significance, and the scientific principles that underpin them.

The Northern Lights occur when charged particles from the sun, known as solar wind, interact with the Earth's magnetic field. The sun constantly emits a stream of charged particles, consisting mostly of electrons and protons, into space. When these solar winds reach the Earth, they collide with the gases in our planet's atmosphere. The Earth's magnetic field, which acts like a shield, directs these particles toward the poles, where the magnetic force is strongest. As these particles collide with the atoms and molecules in the Earth's atmosphere, energy is released in the form of light, creating the breathtaking displays of the aurora.

The colors of the Northern Lights depend on the type of gas in the atmosphere and the altitude at which the particles collide. The most common color is green, which is produced when the charged particles collide with oxygen molecules at altitudes of around 60 miles above the Earth. Red auroras, which are rarer, occur when the particles interact with oxygen at higher altitudes, typically above 150 miles. Nitrogen molecules can produce blue or purple auroras, adding to the variety of colors that can be seen during a particularly strong display. The exact combination of colors, shapes, and patterns in the Northern Lights can vary from one night to the next, making each viewing experience unique.

The movement of the aurora across the sky is influenced by the Earth's magnetic field and the speed of the solar wind. The lights can appear as shimmering curtains, arcs, or rays that stretch across the sky, or they may flicker and dance in seemingly random patterns. Sometimes, the aurora can be faint and subtle, appearing as a soft glow on the horizon, while at other times, it can be a dramatic and intense display that lights up the entire sky. These variations are caused by changes in solar activity, as well as the interaction between the solar wind and the Earth's magnetosphere.

One of the most captivating aspects of the Northern Lights is their unpredictability. Although scientists can predict periods of increased solar activity and the likelihood of auroras occurring, the exact timing, location, and intensity of the display can be difficult to forecast. This sense of mystery adds to the magic of the Northern Lights, as those who are lucky enough to witness them often feel as though they are experiencing something truly special and rare.

The Northern Lights have been a source of wonder and inspiration for people living in the Arctic regions for thousands of years. Indigenous cultures, such as the Inuit and Sami people, have developed rich mythologies and stories to explain the phenomenon. In Inuit culture, one legend suggests that the Northern Lights are the spirits of ancestors playing a game of football in the sky. The flickering and dancing lights represent the movement of the players, and the bright flashes are thought to be the ball being kicked high into the air. Other Inuit myths describe the aurora as the souls of animals, such as whales and seals, illuminating the sky with their light.

The Sami people of Scandinavia also have deep cultural connections to the Northern Lights. In Sami tradition, the lights are believed to be the spirits of the dead, and they are treated with great respect. It was considered dangerous to mock or whistle at the aurora, as doing so could anger the spirits and bring misfortune. The Sami would often use the lights as a way to navigate across the vast, snowy landscapes of the Arctic, relying on the aurora's movement to guide them through the long winter nights. The Northern Lights were not just a natural spectacle for the Sami but a deeply spiritual and practical part of their lives.

In Norse mythology, the aurora was thought to be a reflection of the armor of the Valkyries, the warrior maidens who escorted fallen warriors to the halls of Valhalla. The shimmering lights were seen as a bridge between the mortal world and the realm of the gods, a powerful and mystical connection between the Earth and the heavens. The Vikings, who often sailed under the light of the aurora, regarded the lights as omens, interpreting their movements and colors as messages from the gods.

Across cultures, the Northern Lights have been imbued with deep meaning and significance, reflecting the human need to make sense of the extraordinary and the mysterious. Even today, people continue to find spiritual and emotional connections to the aurora. Modern viewers often describe the experience of witnessing the Northern Lights as deeply humbling, a reminder of the beauty and power of nature, and a moment of awe that connects them to the greater universe.

From a scientific perspective, the study of the Northern Lights has helped researchers better understand the relationship between the Earth and the sun, as well as the behavior of charged particles in the magnetosphere. The field of space weather, which studies the effects of solar activity on the Earth's magnetic field, has important implications for modern technology. For example, solar storms, which can cause particularly strong auroras, have the potential to disrupt satellite communications, GPS systems, and power grids. Understanding the mechanisms behind the aurora and predicting periods of heightened solar activity can help scientists mitigate the impact of these events on our technological infrastructure.

The first scientific explanation for the Northern Lights was proposed in the early 18th century by the Norwegian scientist Kristian Birkeland. Birkeland hypothesized that the aurora was caused by charged particles from the sun interacting with the Earth's magnetic field. His theory was met with skepticism at the time, but it was later confirmed by space missions and satellite observations. Today, Birkeland is recognized as one of the pioneers of auroral research, and his work laid the foundation for much of what we know about the aurora today.

Modern technology has allowed scientists to study the aurora in more detail than ever before. Satellites equipped with specialized instruments can monitor solar activity and the Earth's magnetosphere, providing valuable data on the conditions that lead to the formation of the Northern Lights. Ground-based observatories, often located in remote areas of the Arctic and Antarctic, also play a crucial role in auroral research, capturing stunning images and data that help scientists understand the dynamics of the aurora.

Tourism centered around viewing the Northern Lights has grown significantly in recent years, with travelers from around the world flocking to the Arctic Circle in hopes of witnessing this natural wonder. Countries like Norway, Iceland, Finland, and Canada have become popular destinations for aurora viewing, with many offering guided tours, lodges, and even glass igloos designed to provide the best possible view of the night sky. The allure of the Northern Lights draws people not only for the beauty of the display but also for the chance to experience something that feels truly magical and otherworldly.

While the Northern Lights are visible from many places near the Arctic Circle, such as Alaska, northern Canada, Scandinavia, and Siberia, they can occasionally be seen much farther south during periods of intense solar activity. These rare events allow people in regions as far south as the United States and parts of Europe to catch a glimpse of the aurora, often sparking widespread excitement and fascination.

In conclusion, the Northern Lights are a truly magical phenomenon that combines the beauty of nature with the wonder of the universe. From their origins in solar wind and the Earth's magnetic field to the vibrant colors and shapes they form in the sky, the aurora is a testament to the complexity and power of the natural world. For those who live in the Arctic, the Northern Lights are a familiar part of life, rich in cultural and spiritual significance. For scientists, the aurora offers a fascinating glimpse into the interactions between the sun and our planet, revealing the mysteries of space weather and the forces that shape our world. And for those lucky enough to witness them, the Northern Lights are an unforgettable reminder of the magic and majesty of the Earth's night sky.

Chapter 3: Life of the Inuit People

The Inuit people, known for their remarkable adaptability and deep connection to the harsh Arctic environment, have a rich and fascinating history that spans thousands of years. The term "Inuit" means "the people" in Inuktitut, their native language, and they inhabit the Arctic regions of Canada, Greenland, Alaska, and parts of Siberia. The Inuit have developed a unique way of life that is intrinsically tied to the land, sea, and ice of the Arctic Circle. Understanding the life of the Inuit involves exploring their history, culture, traditional practices, social structures, spirituality, and how they have adapted to modern challenges while maintaining their ancestral traditions.

The Inuit's origins can be traced back over 4,000 years, when their ancestors migrated from Siberia across the Bering Strait to North America. Over generations, they spread across the Arctic, settling in various regions where they could find food and shelter despite the extreme cold and the long winters with little to no daylight. Their ability to survive in such an inhospitable environment is a testament to their resourcefulness, resilience, and deep understanding of the Arctic ecosystem. The Inuit developed tools, clothing, and techniques that enabled them to not only survive but thrive in this environment, and these innovations remain an integral part of their cultural heritage today.

Traditional Inuit life was heavily centered around the seasonal cycles of the Arctic, and their survival depended on hunting, fishing, and gathering. They were nomadic people, moving in small family groups across the tundra, sea ice, and coastline, following the migration patterns of animals. Seals, whales, caribou, and fish were the primary sources of food, and every part of these animals was used to meet their needs. The Inuit practiced sustainable hunting, taking only what they needed and respecting the animals they hunted, which was essential for ensuring that future generations would continue to have enough resources.

Seal hunting was one of the most important activities for the Inuit, as seals provided not only meat but also blubber, which was used for fuel in lamps, and hides, which were used to make waterproof clothing and tents. The Inuit developed sophisticated methods for hunting seals, such as using a harpoon and waiting by breathing holes in the ice, where seals would surface to breathe. Whaling was another significant activity, particularly in regions like Greenland and northern Canada. The Inuit hunted large animals like bowhead and beluga whales, using boats made of seal skins stretched over a wooden frame. Whale hunting was a communal activity, and the meat and blubber were shared among all members of the community, ensuring that everyone had enough food and fuel to survive the long winter months.

Caribou were also a vital resource for the Inuit. These animals migrated in large herds across the tundra, and the Inuit relied on their meat for food and their hides for clothing and shelter. Caribou skins were sewn together to create parkas, boots, and other garments that were essential for surviving the extreme cold. Inuit clothing was incredibly well-adapted to the Arctic environment, often consisting of multiple layers of fur and skin to trap heat and provide insulation. The use of animal materials was not only practical but also deeply connected to Inuit beliefs, as animals were considered spiritual beings with whom the Inuit had a reciprocal relationship. They believed that animals gave themselves to the hunter in exchange for respect and proper treatment, and this reverence for nature remains a core aspect of Inuit culture.

Inuit tools and technologies were ingeniously crafted from the materials available in their environment. Stone, bone, ivory, and wood were commonly used to make tools for hunting, building, and everyday life. The ulu, a versatile, crescent-shaped knife made from stone or metal, was used by Inuit women for skinning animals, cutting meat, and preparing hides. Inuit men used harpoons, spears, and bows and arrows for hunting, all carefully designed for specific types of prey. The construction of igloos, temporary snow shelters, is one of the most iconic symbols of Inuit ingenuity. Igloos were built from blocks of compacted snow and provided insulation from the wind and cold, allowing the Inuit to stay warm even in the most extreme conditions.

Inuit social structures were centered around family and community, with cooperation and sharing being essential values. The harsh Arctic environment made it necessary for people to work together for survival. Food, tools, and resources were shared among family members and the wider community to ensure that no one went without. Leadership in Inuit society was not based on wealth or power but on skills, wisdom, and the ability to provide for others. Elders were highly respected for their knowledge of the land, weather, animals, and traditional practices, and their guidance was crucial for making important decisions about hunting, travel, and community life.

Inuit spirituality and worldview were deeply connected to the natural world and the animals they relied upon for survival. They believed that everything in nature, including animals, plants, and even the land and sea, had a spirit. This belief system, often referred to as animism, shaped their relationship with their environment and guided their behaviors and customs. Hunters performed rituals to show respect for the animals they killed, believing that this respect would ensure the animal's spirit would be reborn and continue to provide for future generations. The shaman, or angakkuq, was a spiritual leader in Inuit communities who acted as a mediator between the human and spirit worlds. Shamans performed ceremonies, healed the sick, and interpreted omens and dreams to protect the community from harm and maintain harmony with the natural world.

Seasonal festivals and gatherings were an important aspect of Inuit life, providing opportunities for socializing, storytelling, and the transmission of knowledge from one generation to the next. Inuit oral traditions are rich with legends, songs, and stories that explain the origins of the world, the behavior of animals, and the lessons of life. Storytelling was a way of passing down wisdom, history, and moral values to children and young people, ensuring that the collective knowledge of the community was preserved. Inuit art, including carvings, drawings, and beadwork, is another way in which they express their connection to the land, animals, and spiritual beliefs. Traditional Inuit art often depicts animals like seals, polar bears, and whales, as well as scenes from daily life and mythological figures, reflecting the deep interconnection between the Inuit and their environment.

The Inuit have faced significant challenges in the modern era, particularly due to the effects of colonization, the introduction of Western technologies, and climate change. In the late 19th and early 20th centuries, European explorers, traders, and missionaries began to make contact with the Inuit, bringing new tools, weapons, and goods, but also diseases and a disruption to traditional ways of life. The establishment of trading posts and missions changed the economic and social structures of Inuit communities, as they became increasingly reliant on trade with outsiders. In some areas, Inuit were encouraged or forced to abandon their nomadic lifestyle and settle in permanent villages, which had profound effects on their culture and identity.

The introduction of Western education systems, Christianity, and government policies further eroded traditional Inuit culture. Inuit children were often sent to residential schools, where they were forbidden from speaking their language or practicing their customs. This loss of cultural continuity had a devastating impact on many Inuit communities, leading to social problems, loss of identity, and a disconnection from their heritage. However, in recent decades, the Inuit have made significant efforts to reclaim and revitalize their language, traditions, and way of life. Indigenous rights movements, cultural programs, and language preservation initiatives have played a crucial role in helping the Inuit regain control of their cultural destiny.

Climate change poses a particularly acute threat to the Inuit, as the Arctic is warming at more than twice the rate of the global average. The melting of sea ice, rising temperatures, and changes in animal migration patterns have made it increasingly difficult for the Inuit to maintain their traditional way of life. Sea ice is essential for hunting seals and whales, and its decline has forced many Inuit hunters to travel farther and take greater risks to find food. Changes in the environment have also affected the availability of fresh water, the health of fish stocks, and the stability of coastal communities.

Despite these challenges, the Inuit continue to show incredible resilience and adaptability. Many Inuit communities are at the forefront of environmental conservation efforts, working to protect the Arctic ecosystem and ensure the sustainability of their traditional practices. The Inuit have also embraced modern technologies in ways that complement their traditional knowledge, using GPS, snowmobiles, and communication tools to aid in hunting, travel, and community building. Inuit-led organizations, such as the Inuit Circumpolar Council, advocate for the rights of Indigenous peoples and play a key role in international discussions on climate change, resource management, and Indigenous sovereignty.

Inuit art and culture have gained global recognition in recent years, with Inuit artists, filmmakers, musicians, and writers bringing their unique perspectives to the world stage. Inuit art, especially carvings made from stone, bone, and ivory, is highly prized for its craftsmanship and cultural significance. In addition, modern Inuit filmmakers have created powerful documentaries and feature films that highlight the beauty of their homeland, the struggles of their people, and the enduring strength of their culture. These artistic contributions have helped raise awareness about Inuit culture and the challenges they face, while also celebrating the richness of their heritage.

In conclusion, the life of the Inuit people is a testament to human ingenuity, resilience, and the ability to thrive in one of the most extreme environments on Earth. From their deep spiritual connection to the land and animals to their sophisticated hunting techniques and social structures, the Inuit have developed a culture that is uniquely suited to the Arctic. While they have faced many challenges, both historically and in the modern world, the Inuit continue to preserve and revitalize their traditions, language, and identity. Today, they stand at the crossroads of tradition and modernity, navigating the impacts of climate change, globalization, and cultural transformation with a deep sense of pride in their heritage and a commitment to ensuring the survival of their people and way of life for future generations.

Chapter 4: Arctic Icebergs and Glaciers

Arctic icebergs and glaciers are two of the most magnificent and iconic natural features of the polar regions, playing a crucial role in shaping the landscape, regulating the global climate, and supporting diverse ecosystems. The Arctic, a region characterized by extreme cold, vast stretches of ice, and remote wilderness, is home to some of the most massive and awe-inspiring glaciers on the planet. Glaciers are enormous bodies of ice that form over centuries or even millennia as layers of snow compact into dense ice. Icebergs, on the other hand, are large chunks of ice that break off from glaciers and float in the ocean. These frozen giants are not only stunning to behold but are also key players in Earth's environmental systems, influencing sea levels, ocean circulation, and the availability of freshwater. Understanding the formation, behavior, and importance of Arctic glaciers and icebergs requires delving into their physical characteristics, their role in the environment, and the growing threats they face from climate change.

Glaciers are massive, slow-moving rivers of ice that form in areas where snowfall exceeds the rate of melting or sublimation. In the Arctic, glaciers develop over thousands of years as snow accumulates, compresses, and transforms into dense ice. The process begins with snowflakes falling and gradually being buried by subsequent layers of snow. As the snow is buried deeper, the weight of the layers above compresses the snow below, turning it into firn, a granular, intermediate stage between snow and ice. Over time, the firn is further compacted and recrystallized into glacial ice, which is much denser than regular ice because it contains very little air. This dense ice begins to flow under the influence of gravity, moving slowly downhill or outward toward the sea. Glaciers can be hundreds or even thousands of feet thick and cover vast areas of land, such as the Greenland Ice Sheet, one of the largest glaciers in the world.

Arctic glaciers can be classified into several types based on their size, shape, and location. Ice sheets, like those found in Greenland, are massive glaciers that cover entire landmasses, often spreading over thousands of square miles. Ice caps are smaller versions of ice sheets that also cover large areas but are confined to mountain ranges or plateaus. Valley glaciers, or alpine glaciers, form in mountain valleys and flow down toward lower elevations. Tidewater glaciers are another important type of glacier found in the Arctic; these glaciers terminate in the ocean and frequently calve, or break off, into icebergs. The process of calving is one of the main ways that icebergs are created, and it can be dramatic, with enormous chunks of ice falling into the sea and creating massive waves.

Icebergs, the floating chunks of ice that break off from glaciers, are a defining feature of the Arctic seascape. Icebergs vary greatly in size, from small fragments known as "growlers" and "bergy bits" to massive icebergs that can be over 100 feet tall and stretch for miles below the surface of the ocean. Despite their imposing size, only about 10% of an iceberg's mass is visible above the waterline, with the remaining 90% submerged beneath the surface. This characteristic has given rise to the phrase "the tip of the iceberg," reflecting how much of an iceberg remains hidden from view. Icebergs are composed of fresh water, and they gradually melt as they drift through warmer ocean currents, releasing freshwater into the sea.

The formation of icebergs is closely tied to the behavior of tidewater glaciers. As glaciers flow toward the sea, the leading edge, or terminus, is often in contact with seawater, which causes it to weaken and eventually break apart. When large pieces of ice calve off, they form icebergs that drift away from the glacier. The size and frequency of calving events can vary depending on factors such as the glacier's thickness, the temperature of the surrounding water, and the rate of ice flow. Some glaciers, particularly those in Greenland, calve regularly, producing a steady stream of icebergs that float into the North Atlantic Ocean.

One of the most famous areas for iceberg formation is the Ilulissat Icefjord in western Greenland, where the Jakobshavn Glacier calves some of the largest and most numerous icebergs in the Northern Hemisphere. The icebergs produced by the Jakobshavn Glacier are so massive that they can take years to melt as they slowly drift southward into warmer waters. Some of these icebergs are believed to have drifted as far as the North Atlantic shipping lanes, where they pose hazards to ships. In fact, it is widely believed that an iceberg calved from a Greenland glacier was responsible for the sinking of the Titanic in 1912.

The role that Arctic glaciers and icebergs play in regulating global sea levels is one of the most significant aspects of their importance. Glaciers store vast amounts of the planet's freshwater, and when they melt or calve into the sea, they contribute to sea level rise. The Greenland Ice Sheet alone contains enough ice to raise global sea levels by about 7 meters (23 feet) if it were to melt completely. Although such a scenario is unlikely to happen quickly, even small increases in the rate of glacier melt and iceberg calving can have significant effects on coastal communities around the world. Over the past few decades, scientists have observed an alarming increase in the rate at which Arctic glaciers are melting, driven largely by rising global temperatures and warming ocean waters. This accelerated melting is a major contributor to the current rise in global sea levels, which threatens to inundate low-lying coastal areas and disrupt ecosystems.

The melting of Arctic glaciers and the calving of icebergs are also closely linked to changes in ocean circulation patterns. As icebergs melt, they release large amounts of freshwater into the ocean, which can alter the salinity and density of seawater. This, in turn, affects the movement of ocean currents, including the thermohaline circulation, also known as the "global conveyor belt," which plays a critical role in regulating the Earth's climate. The North Atlantic, in particular, is a key region for the global conveyor belt, as cold, dense water sinks in this area and drives the circulation of ocean currents around the world. However, the influx of freshwater from melting glaciers and icebergs can disrupt this process, potentially slowing down or even halting the conveyor belt. Such a disruption could have far-reaching consequences for global weather patterns, including changes in temperature, precipitation, and storm activity.

The Arctic ecosystem, which includes a variety of marine and terrestrial species, is highly dependent on the presence of icebergs and glaciers. Many animals, such as polar bears, seals, and walruses, rely on sea ice for hunting, resting, and breeding. Glaciers also provide habitat for microorganisms and algae, which form the base of the food chain in polar regions. As glaciers melt and retreat, they release nutrients into the ocean, which support the growth of phytoplankton, the foundation of the marine food web. However, the rapid melting of glaciers and the decline of sea ice are threatening the survival of many Arctic species, as their habitats shrink and the availability of food decreases.

For the Inuit and other Indigenous peoples of the Arctic, glaciers and icebergs are not only part of the natural landscape but also integral to their way of life. For centuries, these communities have relied on the ice for hunting, fishing, and transportation. The presence of sea ice, which forms from frozen seawater rather than from glaciers, creates pathways for travel across the frozen ocean and provides access to hunting grounds for seals, whales, and other marine animals. The Inuit have developed sophisticated knowledge of the ice, understanding its movements, thickness, and behavior, which has allowed them to survive and thrive in this extreme environment. However, the rapid melting of glaciers and the loss of sea ice due to climate change are disrupting traditional ways of life for many Arctic communities, making it more difficult to hunt, fish, and travel across the ice.

Climate change is the greatest threat facing Arctic glaciers and icebergs today. The Arctic is warming at more than twice the rate of the global average, a phenomenon known as Arctic amplification. This rapid warming is causing glaciers to melt at an unprecedented rate, leading to the retreat of ice sheets, the thinning of glaciers, and the calving of more icebergs. In Greenland, for example, satellite data has shown that the Greenland Ice Sheet is losing more than 250 billion tons of ice each year, contributing to global sea level rise. The accelerated melting of glaciers in the Arctic is not only a symptom of climate change but also a driver of further warming. As glaciers melt, they expose dark land and ocean surfaces that absorb more heat from the sun, amplifying the warming effect in a feedback loop known as the ice-albedo effect.

The loss of Arctic ice has profound implications for global climate systems. As glaciers and sea ice disappear, the Arctic Ocean absorbs more solar radiation, leading to warmer ocean temperatures. This, in turn, affects weather patterns around the world, contributing to more extreme weather events such as heatwaves, storms, and droughts. The melting of permafrost, the frozen soil that covers much of the Arctic, is also releasing large amounts of greenhouse gases, such as methane and carbon dioxide, into the atmosphere, further accelerating global warming.

Efforts to monitor and protect Arctic glaciers and icebergs are underway, with scientists using satellite technology, drones, and remote sensors to study the movement and behavior of ice in the region. These tools provide valuable data on glacier melt rates, iceberg calving events, and changes in sea ice extent, helping researchers better understand the impacts of climate change on the Arctic and the global environment. International agreements, such as the Paris Agreement, aim to limit global warming and reduce greenhouse gas emissions, but the future of the Arctic's glaciers and icebergs remains uncertain.

In conclusion, Arctic icebergs and glaciers are not only strikingly beautiful but also critical components of the Earth's climate system and ecosystems. These frozen giants shape the Arctic landscape, influence ocean circulation, regulate sea levels, and provide habitats for a variety of species. However, the rapid melting of Arctic glaciers and the increasing frequency of iceberg calving due to climate change are causing profound changes in the region, with far-reaching consequences for the planet. As the Arctic continues to warm, the fate of its glaciers and icebergs will play a key role in determining the future of global sea levels, weather patterns, and ecosystems.

Chapter 5: The Midnight Sun Phenomenon

The Midnight Sun phenomenon is one of the most remarkable and unique natural occurrences that take place in the polar regions of the Earth, particularly within the Arctic Circle and the Antarctic Circle. This extraordinary event happens when the sun remains visible for 24 hours a day during certain periods of the year, defying the usual daily cycle of day and night that most people around the world are familiar with. In the Arctic, the Midnight Sun occurs during the summer months, typically from late May to late July, and is a result of the Earth's axial tilt. For the people, animals, and plants living in these high-latitude regions, the Midnight Sun profoundly influences daily life, culture, biology, and the environment. To truly grasp the Midnight Sun phenomenon, it is essential to explore the scientific reasons behind it, its effects on the natural world, and how it has shaped human culture and tradition in these areas.

The Midnight Sun occurs because of the tilt of the Earth's axis, which is inclined at approximately 23.5 degrees relative to its orbit around the sun. This axial tilt means that different parts of the Earth receive varying amounts of sunlight throughout the year. During the summer months, the North Pole is tilted toward the sun, causing the Arctic region to receive continuous daylight for several weeks or even months. As the Earth rotates on its axis, the sun appears to move in a circular path across the sky, but it never dips below the horizon, resulting in 24 hours of sunlight. In contrast, during the winter months, the North Pole is tilted away from the sun, leading to the opposite phenomenon—polar night—when the sun remains below the horizon for an extended period, and darkness prevails.

The closer one is to the poles, the longer the period of the Midnight Sun lasts. For instance, at the Arctic Circle (66.5° N latitude), the

Midnight Sun can be seen for just one day, on the summer solstice around June 21, which is the longest day of the year in the Northern Hemisphere. As one travels further north, the duration of the Midnight Sun increases. At the North Pole itself, the sun remains above the horizon for six months, from the spring equinox in March until the autumn equinox in September. This continuous daylight creates an entirely different experience from the typical day-night cycle, fundamentally altering the way time and light are perceived in the polar regions.

The Midnight Sun has a profound impact on the natural environment, influencing the behavior of animals, the growth of plants, and the overall ecosystem in the Arctic. Animals that inhabit the Arctic region, such as reindeer, arctic foxes, polar bears, and seabirds, have evolved to cope with the unique light conditions brought about by the Midnight Sun. For instance, many migratory birds take advantage of the extended daylight to forage for food around the clock, allowing them to raise their young during the short Arctic summer when food is plentiful. Species like the Arctic tern, which migrates from the Antarctic to the Arctic to breed, benefit from the abundant sunlight to build up their energy reserves for the long journey back south.

Reindeer, which are native to the Arctic, display fascinating behavioral adaptations to the Midnight Sun. Instead of adhering to a strict day-night cycle, reindeer have been shown to exhibit irregular sleeping and feeding patterns during the continuous daylight of summer. Without the regular cues of sunrise and sunset, these animals rely on other environmental factors, such as temperature and food availability, to regulate their activity. This ability to adjust their behavior in response to the Midnight Sun allows them to take full advantage of the short Arctic summer to graze and build up fat reserves for the harsh winter months.

For plants, the Midnight Sun provides a critical window of opportunity for growth and reproduction. The Arctic tundra, which is characterized by permafrost and short growing seasons, is home to a variety of hardy plants that have adapted to thrive in extreme conditions. During the summer months, the continuous daylight allows plants to photosynthesize for much longer periods than in other regions of the world. This burst of sunlight, coupled with the relatively mild temperatures of the Arctic summer, enables plants like mosses, lichens, sedges, and dwarf shrubs to grow rapidly. In many cases, plants in the Arctic must complete their entire life cycle—germination, growth, flowering, and seed production—in just a few short months. The Midnight Sun is thus a vital factor in the survival of these species, as it allows them to maximize their exposure to sunlight and store enough energy to withstand the long, dark winter.

In addition to its effects on the natural world, the Midnight Sun has played a significant role in shaping the cultures and traditions of the people who live in the Arctic. Indigenous groups such as the Sami in northern Scandinavia, the Inuit in Greenland, Canada, and Alaska, and the Chukchi in Siberia have long lived in harmony with the cycles of the Arctic environment, including the unique light patterns brought about by the Midnight Sun. These communities have developed ways of life that are deeply intertwined with the rhythms of the Arctic seasons, and the Midnight Sun is often celebrated as a time of abundance, warmth, and renewal.

For the Sami people, who traditionally practice reindeer herding, the Midnight Sun is an important period for ensuring the health and well-being of their herds. During the summer, the Sami move their reindeer to coastal grazing lands, where the animals can feed on the nutrient-rich vegetation that flourishes under the continuous sunlight. The extended daylight hours also allow the Sami to perform essential tasks, such as repairing equipment, building shelters, and preparing for the winter. The Midnight Sun has become a symbol of the Sami's deep connection to the land and their ability to thrive in one of the harshest environments on Earth.

In modern times, the Midnight Sun has also become a major attraction for tourists, drawing visitors from around the world who wish to experience the surreal beauty of continuous daylight. Popular destinations for Midnight Sun tourism include northern Norway, Sweden, Finland, Iceland, and Greenland, where travelers can engage in a variety of outdoor activities that take advantage of the never-setting sun. Hiking, fishing, kayaking, and wildlife watching are all popular pursuits during the Midnight Sun, as the extended daylight provides ample opportunities to explore the natural wonders of the Arctic. Many cities and towns in these regions hold special Midnight Sun festivals, where locals and visitors alike gather to celebrate the endless summer days with music, food, and cultural performances.

In Norway, the city of Tromsø is known as the "Gateway to the Arctic" and is one of the best places to witness the Midnight Sun. From late May to late July, the sun never dips below the horizon, casting a golden glow over the fjords, mountains, and islands that surround the city. Visitors to Tromsø can take advantage of the Midnight Sun to hike up mountains in the middle of the night, go on boat tours to see whales and seals, or simply enjoy the peaceful atmosphere of the Arctic wilderness. The city of Svalbard, located even further north, experiences an even longer period of the Midnight Sun, with continuous daylight lasting from mid-April to late August. Svalbard is one of the northernmost inhabited places in the world, and its remote location makes it an ideal destination for those seeking solitude and a closer connection to nature during the Midnight Sun.

In addition to its impact on tourism and cultural traditions, the Midnight Sun has also been a source of inspiration for artists, writers, and scientists. The endless daylight, with its surreal and dreamlike quality, has been captured in paintings, photographs, and films, where it is often depicted as both beautiful and eerie. For many people, the experience of the Midnight Sun can be disorienting, as the absence of night disrupts the body's natural circadian rhythms. In fact, researchers have studied the effects of the Midnight Sun on sleep patterns and mental health, noting that the continuous exposure to daylight can make it difficult for some people to fall asleep or maintain regular sleep schedules. In contrast, others report feeling energized and more productive during the Midnight Sun, as the extended daylight encourages outdoor activity and social interaction.

The Midnight Sun has also sparked scientific curiosity, particularly in the fields of astronomy and atmospheric science. Observing the behavior of the sun during the Midnight Sun provides valuable insights into the Earth's axial tilt, orbit, and the nature of light in the polar regions. Atmospheric scientists study the unique optical phenomena associated with the Midnight Sun, such as the golden and orange hues that often tint the sky during the Arctic summer. These colors are the result of the sun's low angle in the sky, which causes sunlight to pass through more of the Earth's atmosphere and scatter in different wavelengths. This scattering effect creates the long-lasting, colorful sunsets and sunrises that are characteristic of the Midnight Sun.

The Midnight Sun is not exclusive to the Arctic; it also occurs in the Antarctic during the Southern Hemisphere's summer months, from late November to late January. However, the Antarctic region is largely uninhabited, apart from scientific research stations, making the phenomenon less accessible to the general public. Nonetheless, the Midnight Sun in Antarctica plays a crucial role in the continent's environment, particularly in the seasonal activities of its wildlife. Emperor penguins, for example, use the extended daylight of the Antarctic summer to raise their chicks, while seals and seabirds take advantage of the abundant food sources available during this time.

While the Midnight Sun is a breathtaking natural wonder, it is also a fragile phenomenon that is being affected by climate change. As global temperatures rise, the Arctic is warming at more than twice the rate of the rest of the planet, leading to the melting of glaciers, sea ice, and permafrost. These changes are altering the Arctic landscape and impacting the delicate balance of its ecosystems. The Midnight Sun, which has been a constant presence in the Arctic for millennia, may be affected by these shifts, as the timing and duration of the phenomenon could change in response to the warming climate. Scientists continue to study the implications of climate change for the Arctic and its unique natural phenomena, including the Midnight Sun, in an effort to better understand and mitigate the effects of global warming.

In conclusion, the Midnight Sun phenomenon is a remarkable and awe-inspiring event that highlights the beauty and complexity of the Earth's polar regions. Caused by the tilt of the Earth's axis and the resulting continuous daylight during the summer months, the Midnight Sun profoundly affects the natural world, shaping the behavior of animals, the growth of plants, and the rhythms of life for the people who call the Arctic home. It has also inspired countless cultural traditions, artistic expressions, and scientific studies. The Midnight Sun is a reminder of the incredible diversity of experiences that exist on our planet, and it offers a glimpse into a world where the boundaries between day and night blur, revealing the wonders of the Arctic in all its radiant glory.

Chapter 6: Arctic Ocean Secrets

The Arctic Ocean, the smallest and shallowest of the world's five major oceans, is a place of remarkable beauty, mystery, and scientific significance. It is also the coldest ocean, located largely within the Arctic Circle and surrounded by North America, Europe, and Asia. The Arctic Ocean is unlike any other, with its vast stretches of sea ice, unique wildlife, and extreme environmental conditions. It is a region that holds many secrets, from its hidden underwater landscapes to its role in global climate regulation. The Arctic Ocean has long been a subject of fascination and study for scientists, explorers, and indigenous peoples alike, who have sought to uncover its mysteries and understand its influence on the planet. As we delve deeper into the secrets of the Arctic Ocean, we discover not only its physical characteristics and the life it supports but also the challenges it faces in the context of climate change and human activity.

One of the most striking features of the Arctic Ocean is its extensive sea ice cover. Unlike the other oceans, where the surface is typically open water, large portions of the Arctic Ocean are covered by sea ice, especially during the winter months. This sea ice plays a crucial role in the Arctic ecosystem and in the global climate system. Sea ice forms when seawater freezes, creating a thick layer of ice that floats on the ocean's surface. During the Arctic winter, the sea ice expands, covering an area larger than the entire United States. In the summer, however, much of the ice melts, causing the ice cover to shrink. The seasonal cycle of sea ice growth and melt has profound effects on the ocean's temperature, salinity, and circulation patterns.

The sea ice of the Arctic Ocean acts as a protective barrier, reflecting sunlight and keeping the waters below cool. This reflective quality, known as the albedo effect, helps to regulate the Earth's temperature by preventing too much solar radiation from being absorbed by the ocean. Sea ice is also a crucial habitat for a wide range of Arctic species, including polar bears, seals, and walruses, which rely on the ice for hunting, resting, and breeding. For example, polar bears use sea ice as a platform to hunt seals, their primary prey. The thinning and shrinking of sea ice due to climate change is threatening the survival of these iconic Arctic species, as it reduces their access to food and forces them to travel greater distances in search of ice.

Beneath the sea ice lies the cold, dark waters of the Arctic Ocean, home to a rich and diverse array of marine life. While the surface may appear frozen and inhospitable, the Arctic Ocean supports a complex ecosystem that includes everything from tiny plankton to massive whales. The Arctic marine food web begins with phytoplankton, microscopic plants that thrive in the nutrient-rich waters of the Arctic. These tiny organisms are the foundation of the Arctic food chain, providing energy for zooplankton, small fish, and other marine animals. During the summer months, when the sea ice melts and sunlight penetrates the water, phytoplankton blooms occur, leading to an explosion of life in the Arctic Ocean. These blooms attract larger animals, such as fish, birds, and marine mammals, all of which depend on the abundance of food during the brief Arctic summer.

One of the most remarkable animals in the Arctic Ocean is the narwhal, often referred to as the "unicorn of the sea" because of its long, spiraled tusk. Narwhals are elusive and mysterious creatures that inhabit the icy waters of the Arctic, particularly around Greenland and Canada. Their tusk, which can grow up to 10 feet long, is actually an elongated tooth, and its exact function remains a subject of scientific debate. Some researchers believe the tusk is used in mating displays or social interactions, while others think it may help narwhals sense changes in the environment, such as variations in water temperature or salinity. Despite the mystery surrounding narwhals, they are an important part of the Arctic ecosystem, feeding on fish and squid and serving as prey for predators like orcas and polar bears.

The Arctic Ocean is also home to several species of seals, including ringed seals, bearded seals, and harp seals, all of which are adapted to the extreme cold and icy conditions of the region. Ringed seals, for example, have thick layers of blubber to insulate them from the cold, and they use their sharp claws to create breathing holes in the sea ice. These breathing holes are essential for their survival, as they allow the seals to stay submerged under the ice while still being able to come up for air. Ringed seals are a primary food source for polar bears, and their survival is closely tied to the availability of sea ice. As the ice melts earlier in the season due to warming temperatures, the seals have less time to raise their pups on the ice, making them more vulnerable to predators and environmental changes.

In addition to its diverse marine life, the Arctic Ocean is also home to some of the most extreme and least-explored underwater landscapes on Earth. The ocean floor of the Arctic is made up of a series of underwater ridges, basins, and mountain ranges, some of which are still being studied and mapped by scientists. One of the most significant features of the Arctic Ocean is the Lomonosov Ridge, a massive underwater mountain range that stretches across the ocean from Greenland to Siberia. This ridge plays a crucial role in shaping the ocean's circulation patterns and influencing the movement of water between the Atlantic and Pacific Oceans. Despite its importance, much of the Arctic seafloor remains largely unexplored due to the harsh conditions and the presence of thick sea ice, which makes it difficult to conduct research in the region.

The Arctic Ocean is also home to significant reserves of natural resources, including oil, gas, and minerals. It is estimated that the Arctic contains around 13% of the world's undiscovered oil and 30% of its undiscovered natural gas, making it a region of considerable interest for energy exploration. However, the extraction of these resources presents significant environmental risks, particularly in the fragile and remote Arctic environment. Oil spills, for example, would be extremely difficult to clean up in the icy waters of the Arctic, and the impacts on marine life and ecosystems could be devastating. The melting of sea ice due to climate change is opening up new areas of the Arctic Ocean for potential exploration, but it also raises concerns about the long-term environmental consequences of increased human activity in the region.

One of the most pressing issues facing the Arctic Ocean today is the impact of climate change. The Arctic is warming at more than twice the rate of the global average, a phenomenon known as Arctic amplification. This rapid warming is causing sea ice to melt at an alarming rate, leading to significant changes in the Arctic environment. Over the past few decades, scientists have observed a dramatic decline in both the extent and thickness of Arctic sea ice, with the summer ice cover shrinking to record lows. The loss of sea ice has profound implications for the Arctic ecosystem, as it threatens the survival of species that depend on the ice, alters ocean circulation patterns, and contributes to rising sea levels.

The melting of Arctic sea ice also has a direct impact on global climate systems. As the ice melts, it exposes darker ocean water, which absorbs more heat from the sun, further accelerating the warming of the Arctic. This feedback loop, known as the ice-albedo effect, amplifies the effects of climate change and contributes to more extreme weather patterns around the world. Additionally, the melting of permafrost in the Arctic is releasing large amounts of greenhouse gases, such as methane and carbon dioxide, into the atmosphere, further exacerbating global warming.

The Arctic Ocean is also a critical player in the global ocean circulation system, often referred to as the "global conveyor belt." This system of currents helps regulate the Earth's climate by redistributing heat from the equator to the poles. In the Arctic, cold, dense water sinks to the bottom of the ocean and flows southward, driving the movement of water throughout the world's oceans. However, the influx of freshwater from melting ice is disrupting this process, potentially slowing down the global conveyor belt and altering weather patterns around the world. Scientists are particularly concerned about the potential impact on the North Atlantic Ocean, where the sinking of cold, dense water is a key driver of the global circulation system. If this process is disrupted, it could lead to changes in temperature and precipitation patterns, with far-reaching consequences for agriculture, ecosystems, and human populations.

Despite the challenges facing the Arctic Ocean, it remains a place of incredible beauty and scientific interest. Researchers continue to study the Arctic to better understand its role in the global climate system, the adaptations of its unique wildlife, and the potential for resource exploration. Advances in technology, such as underwater drones and satellite imagery, are helping scientists map the seafloor, monitor sea ice, and track changes in the Arctic environment over time. These efforts are crucial for developing strategies to protect the Arctic and mitigate the impacts of climate change.

Indigenous peoples of the Arctic, such as the Inuit, have lived in harmony with the Arctic Ocean for thousands of years, relying on its resources for their survival. The Inuit have a deep understanding of the Arctic environment, including the behavior of sea ice, the migration patterns of marine animals, and the seasonal cycles of the ocean. For the Inuit, the Arctic Ocean is not just a body of water, but a vital part of their culture, livelihood, and identity. However, the rapid changes occurring in the Arctic due to climate change are threatening their traditional way of life. The melting of sea ice is making it more difficult for the Inuit to hunt, fish, and travel across the ice, while the warming temperatures are altering the distribution of marine animals they rely on for food.

In conclusion, the Arctic Ocean is a place of immense scientific and cultural significance, holding many secrets that continue to captivate researchers, explorers, and indigenous peoples alike. From its vast stretches of sea ice to its diverse marine life and hidden underwater landscapes, the Arctic Ocean is a unique and dynamic environment that plays a crucial role in regulating the Earth's climate and supporting life in the polar regions. However, the rapid changes occurring in the Arctic due to climate change pose significant challenges for the future of the ocean and the species that depend on it. As we continue to explore and study the Arctic Ocean, it is essential that we work to protect this fragile and vital ecosystem, ensuring that its secrets are preserved for future generations.

Chapter 7: Sled Dogs and Their Role

Sled dogs have played an integral and fascinating role in human life, especially in the Arctic and other cold, remote regions of the world, for thousands of years. These remarkable animals are far more than just pets or working animals; they have been partners, companions, and crucial contributors to survival in some of the most challenging environments on Earth. Their strength, stamina, endurance, and unwavering loyalty have made them indispensable in transporting goods, exploring uncharted territories, hunting, and helping humans endure in places where harsh conditions make modern transportation impractical or impossible. The bond between sled dogs and humans is one of cooperation and mutual respect, honed over centuries of shared struggle in the face of extreme cold, snow, and ice. To fully appreciate the role of sled dogs, it's important to delve into their history, the different types of sled dogs, their training, and the unique physical and psychological characteristics that make them ideally suited to their tasks, as well as their roles in exploration, culture, and sport.

The history of sled dogs dates back thousands of years, with archaeological evidence suggesting that dogs have been used to pull sleds in the Arctic for at least 4,000 years. Indigenous peoples of the Arctic, including the Inuit, Chukchi, and Saami, developed highly efficient methods of dog sledding to travel across the vast, snow-covered landscapes of Siberia, Alaska, Canada, and Greenland. These early sled dogs were essential for hunting, transportation, and trade, helping people move supplies, food, and even their entire communities across the frozen tundra. The partnership between humans and dogs was one of survival, as the harsh Arctic winters made it difficult for people to live and travel without the assistance of sled dogs. The dogs, in turn, relied on the humans for food, care, and companionship, creating a deeply symbiotic relationship.

There are several different types of sled dogs, each bred for specific purposes and adapted to the unique environments in which they worked. The most well-known and iconic sled dog breed is the Siberian Husky, a medium-sized dog with a thick double coat, strong muscles, and a high level of endurance. Siberian Huskies were originally bred by the Chukchi people of Siberia for long-distance sledding in extreme cold, and they are known for their ability to work tirelessly for hours or even days at a time. Their friendly and cooperative nature makes them excellent team members, and they have a strong instinct to pull and run, which makes them ideal for sledding.

Another famous sled dog breed is the Alaskan Malamute, one of the oldest and largest Arctic sled dogs. Malamutes are known for their immense strength and stamina, and they were historically used by Inuit people to pull heavy loads over long distances. Unlike the Siberian Husky, which is more suited for speed and endurance, the Alaskan Malamute is a powerful, slow-moving dog capable of pulling substantial weights, making it an ideal choice for freight work and hauling large supplies of food and equipment. Malamutes are highly intelligent and independent, often working in small teams or even alone, and they are known for their strong loyalty to their human companions.

The Samoyed, another breed associated with sledding, originated with the Samoyedic people of Siberia, who used these dogs not only for sledding but also for herding reindeer and providing warmth by sleeping next to them in the cold winter months. Samoyeds are smaller than Malamutes and Huskies but are highly adaptable, friendly, and hardworking. Their thick, white, fluffy coats are a hallmark of the breed, providing protection from the cold and making them well-suited for life in freezing environments. Despite their smaller size, Samoyeds are known for their strength and determination, qualities that make them excellent sled dogs.

One of the lesser-known but equally important sled dog breeds is the Greenland Dog, a hardy and resilient breed native to Greenland. Greenland Dogs are known for their ability to survive in extreme conditions and their close bond with their human handlers. They are primarily used for hunting seals and polar bears and pulling sleds across the ice. Their strength, endurance, and resistance to cold make them highly valued in the Arctic, where they have been used by the Inuit for centuries to navigate the ice-covered landscape.

The training of sled dogs is a meticulous process that begins at a young age. Puppies are gradually introduced to the routines and challenges of sledding through a combination of socialization, physical training, and learning how to work within a team. One of the most critical aspects of sled dog training is teaching them to work together as a cohesive unit, with each dog in the team having a specific role. The lead dog is arguably the most important position in a sled dog team, as this dog is responsible for setting the pace, following commands, and guiding the team through challenging terrain. Lead dogs are typically highly intelligent, confident, and obedient, with an instinct for leadership and problem-solving.

Behind the lead dog are the swing dogs, whose job is to help turn the team around corners and maintain the rhythm of the group. The next set of dogs, known as team dogs, are the powerhouse of the team, providing the bulk of the pulling force. Finally, the wheel dogs, positioned closest to the sled, are typically the strongest and most experienced dogs, responsible for keeping the sled steady and pulling it forward through deep snow or rough ice. Each position in the team requires specific skills, and mushers (sled drivers) carefully select and train their dogs for these roles based on the individual strengths and temperaments of the animals.

In addition to physical training, sled dogs must be conditioned to endure extreme cold, hunger, and fatigue. They are trained to sleep outside in freezing temperatures and are fed high-energy diets to fuel their endurance. During long journeys or races, sled dogs burn a tremendous amount of calories—up to 10,000 calories a day—so their diet is rich in protein and fat to sustain them. Their ability to work in such harsh conditions is a testament to their remarkable physiology. Sled dogs have adapted over millennia to conserve energy, resist frostbite, and maintain their body heat even in temperatures that can drop to minus 50 degrees Fahrenheit (minus 45 degrees Celsius) or lower. Their thick double coats provide insulation against the cold, and their feet are specially adapted to grip the snow and ice.

The use of sled dogs is not limited to transportation or hunting; they have also played a crucial role in some of history's most daring expeditions and explorations. One of the most famous uses of sled dogs was in the early 20th century during expeditions to the North and South Poles. Explorers such as Roald Amundsen and Robert Peary relied on sled dogs to travel across the treacherous polar landscapes, where no other form of transportation was feasible. Amundsen, in particular, credited his successful journey to the South Pole in 1911 to the strength and endurance of his sled dogs, who helped his team cover vast distances in the frozen wilderness.

Sled dogs also played a heroic role in the 1925 serum run to Nome, Alaska, when an outbreak of diphtheria threatened the lives of thousands of people in the remote town. The only way to deliver the life-saving serum to Nome was by dog sled, as harsh winter conditions made other forms of transportation impossible. Over the course of five and a half days, a relay of sled dog teams covered more than 600 miles (965 kilometers), braving blizzards, freezing temperatures, and treacherous ice to deliver the serum. The lead dog on the final leg of the journey, Balto, became a national hero, and a statue of him stands in Central Park, New York City, as a tribute to the bravery and endurance of the sled dogs who saved countless lives.

In addition to their historical and practical significance, sled dogs have become central to modern dog sledding sports, such as sprint racing, mid-distance racing, and long-distance endurance races. The most famous of these races is the Iditarod Trail Sled Dog Race, held annually in Alaska. The Iditarod covers approximately 1,000 miles (1,600 kilometers) of rugged terrain, stretching from Anchorage to Nome, and is considered one of the most grueling endurance races in the world. Mushers and their dog teams face extreme weather conditions, including blizzards, high winds, and subzero temperatures, as they race across mountains, frozen rivers, and dense forests. The race is a celebration of the heritage of sled dog travel in Alaska, and it tests the physical and mental limits of both dogs and mushers.

Another significant sled dog race is the Yukon Quest, which takes place between Fairbanks, Alaska, and Whitehorse, Yukon, Canada. This race, which is even longer and more challenging than the Iditarod, is known for its remote and harsh conditions, with teams often traveling for days without encountering another person or settlement. The Yukon Quest, like the Iditarod, highlights the endurance, skill, and determination of sled dogs and their mushers.

Despite the rise of modern technology and transportation, sled dogs continue to play an important role in many Arctic communities. In remote villages across Alaska, Canada, Greenland, and Siberia, sled dogs are still used for hunting, transportation, and even search and rescue missions. For many indigenous peoples, dog sledding is not just a practical necessity but also a vital part of their cultural heritage. Dog sledding traditions have been passed down through generations, and the relationship between people and their dogs remains a source of pride and identity in these communities.

In conclusion, sled dogs have had a profound impact on human life, particularly in Arctic and sub-Arctic regions where their strength, endurance, and loyalty have made them indispensable companions. From their historical use by indigenous peoples for hunting and transportation to their role in polar exploration and modern sled dog racing, these remarkable animals have shown time and time again that they are more than capable of thriving in some of the world's harshest environments. Their physical and psychological adaptations to cold, combined with the deep bond they form with their human handlers, have made sled dogs true icons of the Arctic. As we look to the future, it is clear that sled dogs will continue to play an important role in the preservation of cultural traditions and the exploration of remote regions, all while inspiring awe and admiration for their incredible capabilities.

Chapter 8: The Tundra Ecosystem

The tundra ecosystem is one of the most extreme and fascinating ecosystems on Earth. Spanning the northernmost regions of the planet, including parts of North America, Europe, and Asia, the tundra is characterized by its harsh climatic conditions, permafrost, short growing seasons, and limited biodiversity. Despite these challenges, the tundra supports a surprising variety of life forms that have evolved remarkable adaptations to survive in such a seemingly inhospitable environment. The tundra is divided into two main types: the Arctic tundra and the alpine tundra, with the Arctic tundra being the most well-known and expansive, stretching across the circumpolar regions surrounding the North Pole.

One of the defining features of the tundra ecosystem is its cold climate. Winters are long, dark, and bitterly cold, with temperatures often plummeting below -40 degrees Celsius (-40 degrees Fahrenheit). Summers are short, cool, and marked by almost constant daylight in the far northern regions, a phenomenon known as the Midnight Sun. The growing season in the tundra lasts only a few weeks, typically from late June to August, during which temperatures may rise to a modest 10-15 degrees Celsius (50-59 degrees Fahrenheit). Precipitation in the tundra is also minimal, with most areas receiving less than 25 centimeters (10 inches) of precipitation per year, often in the form of snow. In this sense, the tundra is sometimes referred to as a "cold desert" due to its low levels of moisture.

One of the most significant factors shaping the tundra ecosystem is permafrost, a layer of permanently frozen ground that can extend hundreds of meters below the surface. Permafrost remains frozen year-round, except for a thin surface layer that thaws during the brief summer months, allowing plants to grow. This surface layer, known as the active layer, varies in thickness depending on the location and climatic conditions. The presence of permafrost has profound effects on the tundra's landscape and vegetation. It prevents the deep rooting of plants, resulting in a unique, low-lying vegetation cover dominated by mosses, lichens, grasses, sedges, and dwarf shrubs. Trees are unable to grow in the tundra due to the shallow active layer and the harsh, wind-swept conditions.

The plant life in the tundra has evolved remarkable adaptations to survive in the cold, nutrient-poor soils and the short growing season. Many tundra plants are low-growing and form dense mats or cushions to conserve heat and resist the strong, drying winds that sweep across the open landscape. These plants often have small, waxy leaves to reduce water loss through transpiration, a crucial adaptation in a region where water is scarce for much of the year. Tundra plants also have shallow root systems that enable them to take advantage of the thawed active layer, absorbing nutrients from the thin, organic-rich soil. Many plants in the tundra have dark-colored leaves and stems, which help them absorb more heat from the sun and raise their temperature slightly above the surrounding air.

Mosses and lichens play a particularly important role in the tundra ecosystem. Mosses are able to thrive in the cold and damp conditions of the tundra, where they form thick carpets that help insulate the soil and retain moisture. Lichens, which are symbiotic associations between fungi and algae or cyanobacteria, are highly resistant to extreme cold and can grow on rocks, soil, and even other plants. They are a critical food source for herbivores such as caribou and reindeer, particularly during the winter months when other food is scarce. Lichens can survive long periods of dormancy and resume growth rapidly once conditions improve, making them well-suited to the unpredictable climate of the tundra.

Despite the limited plant diversity in the tundra, the ecosystem supports a range of herbivores that have adapted to survive in this challenging environment. One of the most iconic tundra herbivores is the caribou (known as reindeer in Eurasia). Caribou are highly migratory animals that travel vast distances in search of food, often moving between the tundra and the boreal forest during different seasons. In the summer, caribou feed on grasses, sedges, and shrubs, while in the winter, they rely on lichens as their primary food source. Their large, concave hooves are adapted for walking on snow and digging through it to reach food, while their thick coats provide insulation against the cold.

Other herbivores in the tundra include the Arctic hare, a species that has evolved to withstand the freezing temperatures with its dense fur and ability to change color from brown in the summer to white in the winter for camouflage against the snow. The Arctic hare feeds on woody plants, mosses, and lichens, and is known for its agility and speed, which help it evade predators such as Arctic foxes and wolves. Lemmings, small rodents that live in burrows beneath the snow, are also a key component of the tundra food web. Lemmings feed on grasses, sedges, and mosses, and their populations fluctuate dramatically from year to year. During peak population years, lemmings provide a crucial food source for predators such as snowy owls, Arctic foxes, and weasels.

The tundra ecosystem is home to several predators that have adapted to life in the extreme cold. One of the most well-known tundra predators is the Arctic fox, a small, highly adaptable carnivore that has evolved to survive in some of the harshest environments on Earth. Arctic foxes have thick fur that changes color with the seasons, from white in the winter to brown or gray in the summer, helping them blend into their surroundings and remain undetected by both prey and predators. They are opportunistic feeders, preying on lemmings, voles, and birds, and scavenging for carrion left behind by larger predators such as polar bears. During lean times, Arctic foxes have been known to store food in caches to survive the long, harsh winters when prey is scarce.

Another apex predator in the tundra is the wolf, particularly the Arctic wolf, a subspecies adapted to the cold and isolation of the far northern regions. Arctic wolves primarily hunt large herbivores such as caribou and musk oxen, working in packs to bring down prey that would be too large for a single wolf to tackle alone. Wolves play a crucial role in the tundra ecosystem by controlling the populations of herbivores, which in turn helps regulate vegetation growth and maintain the balance of the ecosystem. Polar bears, while more closely associated with the sea ice and marine environments, also venture into the tundra during the summer months when the ice melts. These formidable predators rely on their fat reserves and occasionally hunt land animals such as Arctic hares or scavenge for food in the tundra.

Birds are another important group of animals in the tundra ecosystem. During the brief Arctic summer, the tundra becomes a bustling hub of avian activity as millions of migratory birds arrive to breed and raise their young. The tundra's open, treeless landscape provides an ideal habitat for ground-nesting birds, and the abundance of insects during the summer months offers a rich food source for both adults and chicks. Some of the most common bird species in the tundra include snow buntings, lapland longspurs, and ptarmigans, all of which have adapted to the cold climate with specialized plumage and behaviors. The snowy owl, one of the most iconic tundra birds, is a top predator that preys on lemmings and other small mammals. During years when lemming populations are high, snowy owl numbers increase as well, highlighting the interconnectedness of the tundra food web.

The tundra's harsh conditions also pose significant challenges for the animals that live there, particularly during the winter months when food is scarce, and temperatures plummet. Many tundra animals have evolved strategies to cope with these challenges, such as hibernation, migration, or developing specialized physical adaptations. For example, some animals, like the Arctic ground squirrel, hibernate during the winter to conserve energy and avoid the harshest conditions. Others, like caribou and migratory birds, move to warmer areas during the winter and return to the tundra in the summer when food is more abundant.

In addition to its unique wildlife, the tundra is also home to indigenous peoples who have lived in and adapted to the extreme conditions of the region for thousands of years. The Inuit, Saami, and Nenets are among the indigenous groups that inhabit the Arctic tundra, relying on traditional knowledge and practices to survive in this challenging environment. These communities have developed sustainable ways of living that are closely tied to the land and its resources. For example, reindeer herding is a central part of Saami culture, while the Inuit have traditionally relied on hunting marine mammals such as seals and whales for food, clothing, and fuel. The indigenous peoples of the tundra have a deep understanding of the ecosystem and have developed cultural practices that reflect their close relationship with the land and its wildlife.

Despite the tundra's remote location and seemingly untouchable nature, it is increasingly under threat from human activities and climate change. One of the most significant impacts of climate change on the tundra is the thawing of permafrost. As global temperatures rise, the permafrost is beginning to melt, releasing large amounts of stored carbon in the form of methane and carbon dioxide into the atmosphere. This release of greenhouse gases further accelerates global warming in a positive feedback loop, contributing to the rapid warming of the Arctic. The thawing of permafrost also destabilizes the ground, leading to erosion, the collapse of infrastructure, and changes in the hydrology of the region. For the indigenous peoples and wildlife of the tundra, these changes pose significant challenges, as the ecosystems they rely on are disrupted.

Another major threat to the tundra ecosystem is resource extraction, particularly oil and gas drilling. The Arctic tundra is rich in natural resources, and as ice melts and new areas become accessible, there is increasing interest in exploiting these resources. However, drilling and mining activities can cause widespread damage to the fragile tundra landscape, destroying habitats and disrupting wildlife populations. The construction of roads, pipelines, and other infrastructure also fragments the ecosystem and can lead to pollution and habitat loss.

Conservation efforts in the tundra are essential to protect this unique and fragile ecosystem. Protected areas such as national parks and wildlife refuges play a critical role in preserving the tundra's biodiversity and ensuring that both wildlife and indigenous peoples can continue to thrive. International cooperation is also vital, as the Arctic is a shared region that requires coordinated efforts to address the challenges posed by climate change, resource extraction, and habitat degradation.

In conclusion, the tundra ecosystem is a remarkable and resilient environment that supports a diverse array of plant and animal life despite its harsh conditions. The adaptations of tundra species to the cold, low-nutrient soils, and short growing seasons are a testament to the power of evolution and the ability of life to thrive in even the most extreme environments. However, the tundra is also a fragile ecosystem that is highly vulnerable to the impacts of climate change and human activities. Protecting the tundra and its inhabitants requires a deep understanding of the ecosystem's complexities and a commitment to preserving its unique characteristics for future generations. As we continue to study and explore the tundra, we must also take action to mitigate the effects of climate change and ensure that this incredible ecosystem remains a vital part of our planet's biodiversity.

Chapter 9: Arctic Foxes and Their Adaptations

Arctic foxes are fascinating creatures that have evolved a wide range of remarkable adaptations that allow them to survive in one of the harshest environments on Earth—the Arctic tundra. These small, resilient animals are perfectly suited to the extreme cold, limited food supply, and seasonal changes of the far north. Their physical traits, hunting strategies, social behavior, and ability to adapt to changing environmental conditions make them one of the most iconic and successful species in the Arctic. Understanding the adaptations of Arctic foxes requires a closer look at their physical characteristics, feeding habits, seasonal behaviors, and how they cope with the changing climate and environmental challenges that threaten their survival.

One of the most striking and well-known adaptations of the Arctic fox is its thick, multi-layered fur coat, which provides insulation and protection against the frigid temperatures of the Arctic. In fact, the Arctic fox has one of the warmest fur coats of any animal in the world, enabling it to withstand temperatures as low as -50 degrees Celsius (-58 degrees Fahrenheit) or even lower. The fur is made up of two layers: a dense, soft undercoat that traps heat close to the body, and a longer, outer layer of guard hairs that protect the fox from wind, snow, and moisture. During the winter, the Arctic fox's fur changes to a brilliant white color, providing perfect camouflage against the snow and ice, which helps it avoid predators and hunt more effectively. In the summer, the fur sheds and changes to a brown or gray color, blending in with the tundra's rocky, snowless landscape. This seasonal camouflage is critical for the fox's survival, as it relies on stealth and surprise when hunting small prey like lemmings, voles, and birds.

In addition to its fur, the Arctic fox has several other physical adaptations that help it conserve heat and energy in the cold Arctic climate. Its small, compact body shape is one of these adaptations. The Arctic fox has relatively short legs, ears, and muzzle compared to other fox species, which reduces its surface area and minimizes heat loss. This is an example of what is known as Bergmann's rule, which states that animals in colder climates tend to have more compact body shapes to conserve body heat. The Arctic fox's short, rounded ears are especially important for preventing heat loss, as they reduce the amount of exposed skin that could be vulnerable to frostbite.

The Arctic fox's paws are another key adaptation to its icy environment. The bottoms of the fox's feet are covered in dense fur, which helps insulate them from the cold ground and prevents the animal from slipping on ice. This feature, known as furred footpads, is unique to Arctic foxes and a few other Arctic animals. The fur on their paws also gives them traction on snow and ice, allowing them to move quickly and easily across the frozen landscape. Additionally, Arctic foxes have sharp, curved claws that help them dig through snow and ice to find food, build dens, or escape predators.

Thermoregulation, or the ability to maintain a stable internal body temperature, is another critical adaptation of the Arctic fox. Unlike many animals that hibernate or migrate to escape the cold, Arctic foxes remain active throughout the winter, even during the darkest, coldest months. To do this, they have developed an impressive ability to regulate their body temperature. Their metabolic rate increases in cold weather, helping them generate extra body heat. When temperatures drop significantly, Arctic foxes curl up into tight balls, tucking their noses and feet under their bodies and wrapping their thick, bushy tails around themselves for added insulation. This behavior helps reduce heat loss and allows the fox to conserve energy during long periods of inactivity or harsh weather.

Another key to the Arctic fox's survival is its highly adaptable diet. In the tundra, food sources can be scarce and unpredictable, especially during the winter months when snow covers the ground and many animals hibernate or migrate south. The primary food source for Arctic foxes is small mammals, particularly lemmings, which are abundant in the Arctic and experience dramatic population booms and busts in cycles of three to five years. When lemmings are plentiful, Arctic foxes will hunt them almost exclusively, but when lemming populations crash, the foxes must rely on a more varied diet. They are opportunistic feeders and will eat almost anything they can find, including birds, eggs, fish, carrion, berries, and even seaweed. In coastal areas, Arctic foxes will scavenge the remains of marine animals such as seals or fish that wash up on shore, and they have been known to follow polar bears to feed on leftover scraps from the bears' kills.

During the summer months, Arctic foxes take advantage of the brief period of abundance in the tundra. They actively hunt birds and small mammals, and they also store food to prepare for the long winter ahead. Arctic foxes are known for their caching behavior, in which they bury excess food in the ground or snow to eat later when resources become scarce. This behavior is particularly important for survival in the winter, when hunting becomes more difficult and food is harder to find. The foxes have an incredible memory for locating their food caches, and they will often dig them up months later when needed. This food storage strategy is a critical adaptation that helps them survive the harsh winter months when food is otherwise scarce.

Reproduction and parental care are also important aspects of the Arctic fox's life cycle that reflect its adaptation to the extreme environment. Arctic foxes mate once a year, usually in late winter or early spring. The timing of their reproductive cycle is closely tied to the availability of food, as the foxes need to ensure that there will be enough resources to feed their young during the summer. The gestation period for Arctic foxes is around 50 days, and the females typically give birth to a litter of 5 to 10 pups, although larger litters of up to 14 pups are not uncommon. The size of the litter is often dependent on the availability of food, with larger litters being born in years when lemming populations are high.

Arctic foxes are attentive and caring parents. Both the mother and father share in the responsibility of raising the pups, with the male providing food for the female while she nurses the young in the den. The dens themselves are another fascinating adaptation of the Arctic fox. These dens are often complex underground burrows that can have multiple entrances and chambers, providing shelter from predators and protection from the elements. Some Arctic fox dens are passed down through generations and may be used for many years. The dens are usually located in areas with good visibility, such as hillsides or ridges, where the foxes can keep an eye out for potential threats.

The pups are born blind and helpless, but they grow rapidly, and by the time they are around three weeks old, they begin to explore outside the den. The parents continue to provide food for the pups until they are old enough to hunt on their own, usually by the time they are around three to four months old. By the end of the summer, the young foxes are fully grown and ready to face the challenges of the Arctic winter.

Social behavior among Arctic foxes can vary depending on food availability and environmental conditions. While some Arctic foxes are solitary animals, others form small family groups, especially during the breeding season. In areas with high food availability, such as near bird colonies or where marine resources are abundant, Arctic foxes may form loose colonies, with multiple families living in close proximity to each other. In contrast, in regions where food is scarce, Arctic foxes tend to be more territorial and solitary, defending their food caches and hunting grounds from intruders.

One of the biggest challenges facing Arctic foxes today is climate change, which is rapidly altering the environment of the Arctic. As temperatures rise, the tundra is warming at an unprecedented rate, causing significant changes to the landscape, vegetation, and wildlife. One of the most immediate effects of climate change on Arctic foxes is the shrinking of their habitat. As the Arctic warms, the treeline is gradually moving north, and forests are encroaching on the tundra. This is allowing red foxes, a larger and more aggressive species, to expand their range into areas that were once the exclusive territory of Arctic foxes. Red foxes are stronger competitors for food and are known to attack and kill Arctic foxes, putting additional pressure on their populations.

Another consequence of climate change is the disruption of the lemming population cycles, which are closely tied to snow cover and seasonal weather patterns. Warmer winters with less snow can lead to lower lemming populations, which in turn affects the food supply for Arctic foxes. In years when lemming populations are low, Arctic foxes may struggle to find enough food to survive and reproduce. Additionally, the melting of sea ice is reducing the availability of marine resources, such as seal carcasses, which Arctic foxes rely on in coastal areas.

Conservation efforts are underway to protect Arctic fox populations and their habitat. Several countries have established protected areas in the Arctic to safeguard critical tundra ecosystems and the wildlife that depends on them. In addition, researchers are studying the effects of climate change on Arctic fox populations and working to develop strategies to mitigate its impact. One of the key goals of conservation efforts is to ensure that Arctic foxes have access to sufficient food and habitat to support healthy populations, even as the environment changes.

In conclusion, Arctic foxes are remarkable animals that have evolved a wide range of adaptations to survive in the extreme conditions of the Arctic tundra. Their thick fur, compact bodies, furred footpads, and ability to store food for the winter all contribute to their success in this harsh environment. Their opportunistic feeding habits and ability to cache food allow them to survive even when resources are scarce, while their social behavior and parental care ensure the survival of their young in a challenging world. However, the future of Arctic foxes is uncertain as they face new threats from climate change, habitat loss, and competition with red foxes. Despite these challenges, the resilience and adaptability of the Arctic fox give hope that this iconic species will continue to thrive in the Arctic for generations to come.

Chapter 10: The Impact of Climate Change

The impact of climate change is one of the most pressing and far-reaching challenges facing the world today. It is a global issue that affects not just the environment, but also human health, economies, and social structures. Climate change refers to long-term alterations in temperature, precipitation, and other atmospheric conditions caused primarily by human activities, particularly the burning of fossil fuels such as coal, oil, and natural gas. These activities release greenhouse gases, such as carbon dioxide (CO_2), methane (CH_4), and nitrous oxide (N_2O), into the atmosphere, where they trap heat and cause the Earth's temperature to rise, a phenomenon known as the greenhouse effect. While the Earth's climate has always experienced natural fluctuations, the rapid pace and scale of current changes are unprecedented in human history. These changes are having profound and often destructive effects on ecosystems, weather patterns, sea levels, and biodiversity, and they pose significant risks to human societies, particularly those in vulnerable regions.

One of the most visible and well-documented impacts of climate change is the rise in global temperatures. Since the late 19th century, the Earth's average surface temperature has increased by approximately 1.1 degrees Celsius (2 degrees Fahrenheit), with most of this warming occurring in the past few decades. This rise in temperature is having wide-ranging consequences across the planet. The most dramatic temperature increases are occurring in the Arctic, where the phenomenon known as Arctic amplification causes warming at rates two to three times faster than the global average. This warming is causing the polar ice caps and glaciers to melt at an alarming rate, contributing to rising sea levels and the loss of critical habitats for animals such as polar bears, seals, and walruses.

Melting ice and rising sea levels are among the most immediate and dangerous effects of climate change. As glaciers and ice sheets in Greenland, Antarctica, and the Arctic melt, they release massive amounts of freshwater into the oceans. In addition, the thermal expansion of seawater (water expands as it warms) contributes to the rise in sea levels. Over the past century, global sea levels have risen by about 20 centimeters (8 inches), and they are projected to rise by another 0.3 to 1.2 meters (1 to 4 feet) by the end of this century, depending on the level of future greenhouse gas emissions. Rising sea levels pose a severe threat to coastal communities around the world, particularly in low-lying regions such as the Maldives, Bangladesh, and parts of the United States, where millions of people live in areas at risk of flooding. In addition to inundating homes and infrastructure, rising seas also lead to the erosion of coastlines, saltwater intrusion into freshwater aquifers, and the loss of wetlands, which are crucial for biodiversity and flood protection.

The warming of the Earth's climate is also altering weather patterns, leading to more extreme and unpredictable weather events. Heatwaves, droughts, hurricanes, and heavy rainfall events are becoming more frequent and intense as a result of climate change. For example, heatwaves are occurring more often and lasting longer, putting strain on public health systems and increasing the risk of heat-related illnesses and deaths, particularly among vulnerable populations such as the elderly, children, and those with pre-existing health conditions. In 2021, a record-breaking heatwave in the Pacific Northwest of the United States and Canada caused temperatures to soar to over 49 degrees Celsius (120 degrees Fahrenheit), leading to hundreds of deaths and devastating wildfires.

Droughts are also becoming more severe in many parts of the world, particularly in regions that are already prone to water scarcity, such as sub-Saharan Africa, the Middle East, and parts of the western United States. Prolonged droughts can have devastating effects on agriculture, leading to crop failures, food shortages, and economic hardship for farmers and rural communities. In some cases, droughts have contributed to conflicts over water resources, exacerbating political instability and forcing people to migrate in search of more hospitable living conditions. For example, the prolonged drought in Syria from 2006 to 2010 is believed to have contributed to the country's civil war by displacing rural populations and increasing tensions over scarce resources.

At the same time, climate change is also increasing the frequency and intensity of heavy rainfall events, which can lead to flooding and landslides. Warmer air holds more moisture, which means that storms have the potential to produce more rain. This has been particularly evident in recent years with storms such as Hurricane Harvey in 2017, which dumped more than 60 inches of rain on parts of Texas, causing catastrophic flooding and billions of dollars in damage. Similarly, extreme rainfall events have led to devastating floods in countries such as India, Pakistan, and Germany, where thousands of people have been displaced from their homes.

Changes in weather patterns are also disrupting ecosystems and biodiversity. As temperatures rise, many species are being forced to migrate to new areas in search of suitable habitats. For example, some species of birds, fish, and insects are moving toward the poles or to higher elevations where temperatures are cooler. However, not all species are able to adapt or migrate, and many are facing the risk of extinction as their habitats become increasingly inhospitable. The loss of Arctic sea ice, for example, is threatening the survival of polar bears, which rely on the ice to hunt for seals. Coral reefs, which are among the most biodiverse ecosystems on Earth, are also under threat from warming ocean temperatures and ocean acidification, which is caused by the absorption of excess CO_2 by seawater. Coral bleaching, a phenomenon in which corals lose their vibrant colors and become more susceptible to disease, has become more frequent in recent decades, with devastating effects on marine life that depend on coral reefs for food and shelter.

Ocean acidification is another significant impact of climate change that is often overlooked. As the oceans absorb more CO2 from the atmosphere, the water becomes more acidic, which can have harmful effects on marine organisms, particularly those that rely on calcium carbonate to build their shells and skeletons, such as mollusks, crabs, and coral. Acidification weakens these organisms and makes it harder for them to survive, which in turn affects the entire marine food chain, including fish populations that are vital to human livelihoods and food security.

Climate change also has profound implications for agriculture and food security. Changes in temperature, precipitation patterns, and the frequency of extreme weather events can disrupt crop production, leading to lower yields and higher food prices. In some regions, crops may no longer be able to grow due to shifts in climate zones. For example, rising temperatures are expected to reduce the productivity of staple crops such as wheat, rice, and maize in many parts of the world, particularly in tropical and subtropical regions where food insecurity is already a pressing issue. In contrast, some regions, such as parts of northern Europe and Canada, may see temporary increases in agricultural productivity due to longer growing seasons, but these gains are likely to be offset by other negative impacts, such as water scarcity and soil degradation.

In addition to threatening food security, climate change is also impacting global water resources. Changes in precipitation patterns, coupled with the melting of glaciers and snowpacks, are altering the availability of freshwater in many parts of the world. In areas that depend on glacial meltwater for drinking water, irrigation, and hydropower, such as the Andes, the Himalayas, and the Alps, the retreat of glaciers is leading to reduced water supplies. At the same time, rising temperatures are increasing evaporation rates, further reducing the amount of available freshwater in already dry regions. This is particularly concerning in places such as the Middle East and North Africa, where water scarcity is already a critical issue and is expected to worsen as climate change progresses.

The impacts of climate change are not limited to the natural environment; they also have far-reaching social, economic, and political consequences. Climate change is a "threat multiplier" that exacerbates existing inequalities and vulnerabilities. It disproportionately affects marginalized communities, including low-income populations, indigenous peoples, and those living in developing countries, who often have fewer resources to cope with the effects of climate change. For example, small island nations such as Kiribati, Tuvalu, and the Marshall Islands are at risk of disappearing entirely due to rising sea levels, and many of their residents may be forced to migrate to other countries as climate refugees. In some cases, the displacement of people due to climate change-related events, such as floods, droughts, and hurricanes, can lead to increased tension and conflict over resources in receiving areas.

In response to these growing threats, governments, organizations, and individuals around the world are taking action to mitigate the effects of climate change and adapt to its impacts. International efforts, such as the Paris Agreement, aim to limit global warming to well below 2 degrees Celsius above pre-industrial levels, with an aspirational goal of limiting warming to 1.5 degrees Celsius. Achieving this goal requires a rapid transition away from fossil fuels and toward renewable energy sources, such as wind, solar, and hydropower, as well as efforts to reduce deforestation, promote energy efficiency, and invest in carbon capture and storage technologies.

Adaptation strategies are also crucial for helping communities cope with the impacts of climate change. These strategies include building more resilient infrastructure, such as flood defenses and drought-resistant agriculture, as well as improving early warning systems for extreme weather events. In some cases, adaptation may also involve relocating vulnerable communities or restoring natural ecosystems, such as wetlands and mangroves, which can provide protection against storm surges and flooding.

While progress is being made, the scale of the challenge posed by climate change is immense, and much more needs to be done to address its root causes and protect both people and the planet. The science is clear: the longer we delay action, the more severe the consequences will be. However, the solutions to climate change are within our reach, and by working together on a global scale, we can reduce greenhouse gas emissions, protect ecosystems, and build a more sustainable and resilient future for all.

Chapter 11: Arctic Exploration History

The history of Arctic exploration is a tale of human courage, ambition, and perseverance. Spanning centuries, this story chronicles the quest to explore, map, and understand one of the most remote and unforgiving regions of the planet—the Arctic. The motivations for Arctic exploration have evolved over time, from the pursuit of new trade routes and territorial expansion to scientific discovery and national prestige. Throughout history, explorers faced tremendous challenges, including extreme cold, unpredictable weather, treacherous ice, and dangerous wildlife. Many expeditions ended in failure or tragedy, but the knowledge and discoveries gained from Arctic exploration have significantly advanced our understanding of this unique and remote part of the world.

The first recorded encounters with the Arctic date back thousands of years, when indigenous peoples, such as the Inuit, Sami, and Chukchi, made their homes in the region. These early inhabitants developed remarkable adaptations to survive in the harsh Arctic environment, including specialized clothing, tools, and hunting techniques. Their knowledge of the land, sea, and ice, passed down through generations, would later prove invaluable to European explorers who ventured into the Arctic in search of new trade routes and wealth. For these indigenous groups, the Arctic was not an unexplored wilderness but a well-known and navigable landscape. However, European exploration of the Arctic began in earnest during the Age of Discovery, as nations sought to expand their influence and find new routes to Asia.

The quest for the Northwest Passage, a fabled sea route through the Arctic connecting the Atlantic and Pacific Oceans, was one of the primary drivers of early Arctic exploration. European explorers, particularly from England and the Netherlands, believed that finding this passage would provide a shorter and more efficient route to the lucrative markets of Asia, bypassing the long and dangerous voyage around the southern tip of Africa or South America. The search for the Northwest Passage began in the late 15th and early 16th centuries, with explorers such as John Cabot and Martin Frobisher leading early expeditions. However, these early voyages were hindered by the treacherous conditions of the Arctic, including thick sea ice, freezing temperatures, and a lack of accurate maps or knowledge of the region.

One of the most famous early Arctic explorers was Sir John Franklin, a British naval officer who led several expeditions to the Arctic in the early 19th century. Franklin's final expedition, launched in 1845, aimed to navigate and chart the Northwest Passage. He commanded two ships, the HMS Erebus and the HMS Terror, with a crew of 129 men. The expedition was well-provisioned and equipped with the latest technology, including steam engines to help break through ice. However, despite these advantages, Franklin's expedition ended in disaster. Both ships became trapped in the ice, and the entire crew perished. The fate of the Franklin expedition remained a mystery for many years, but later searches uncovered artifacts, human remains, and Inuit testimony that helped piece together the tragic story. It is now believed that the crew succumbed to a combination of scurvy, starvation, and exposure after abandoning their icebound ships and attempting to trek south on foot. The Franklin expedition remains one of the most infamous and tragic episodes in the history of Arctic exploration.

Despite the many failures and tragedies associated with the search for the Northwest Passage, explorers continued to venture into the Arctic throughout the 19th and early 20th centuries. Some, like Robert McClure and John Rae, made significant discoveries and contributions to Arctic exploration. In 1850, McClure, a British naval officer, successfully traversed the Northwest Passage from west to east, although much of his journey was made on foot and by sled rather than by ship. Rae, a Scottish explorer, was one of the first Europeans to recognize the value of Inuit survival techniques, and he relied on their knowledge to survive and map large portions of the Canadian Arctic. Rae's reports of the Franklin expedition's demise, based on Inuit accounts, were initially dismissed by the British public but were later proven accurate.

While the search for the Northwest Passage dominated much of early Arctic exploration, explorers were also drawn to the North Pole, the ultimate symbol of human ambition and conquest. Reaching the geographic North Pole, located in the middle of the Arctic Ocean, posed a unique set of challenges. Unlike the South Pole, which sits on a solid landmass, the North Pole is located on ever-shifting sea ice, making it difficult to access and navigate. Numerous attempts to reach the North Pole were made throughout the 19th century, but it was not until the early 20th century that explorers finally succeeded.

One of the most famous and controversial figures in the race to the North Pole was American explorer Robert Peary. Peary claimed to have reached the North Pole on April 6, 1909, accompanied by his assistant Matthew Henson and a team of Inuit guides. However, Peary's claim was met with skepticism, and it remains disputed to this day. Peary's rival, Dr. Frederick Cook, also claimed to have reached the North Pole a year earlier in 1908, but his claim was widely discredited after an investigation by the National Geographic Society. Despite the controversy, Peary's expedition is generally recognized as the first to reach the North Pole, although modern analyses of his records and calculations suggest that he may have fallen short by several miles.

The early 20th century also saw significant advances in Arctic exploration by air. In 1926, Norwegian explorer Roald Amundsen, who had previously become the first person to reach the South Pole, led an expedition to the North Pole by airship. Amundsen and his team flew over the North Pole in the airship *Norge*, marking the first confirmed sighting of the pole by humans. Amundsen's expedition was a significant milestone in the history of Arctic exploration, demonstrating the potential of air travel to overcome the challenges posed by the Arctic's ice and isolation.

The Soviet Union also played a major role in Arctic exploration during the early 20th century. In the 1930s, Soviet explorers and scientists undertook extensive expeditions to map and study the Arctic, particularly the vast and remote Siberian Arctic coastline. One of the most ambitious Soviet projects was the establishment of drifting ice stations, where scientists lived and conducted research on floating ice floes for extended periods. These ice stations provided valuable data on Arctic oceanography, meteorology, and sea ice dynamics, contributing to a greater understanding of the Arctic environment.

In addition to territorial and scientific motives, Arctic exploration also became a matter of national pride and prestige during the Cold War era. Both the United States and the Soviet Union saw the Arctic as a strategically important region, not only for its natural resources but also for its potential as a theater of military operations. The Arctic Ocean became a focal point for submarine activity, with both superpowers deploying nuclear submarines beneath the ice. In 1958, the U.S. submarine *USS Nautilus* became the first vessel to travel beneath the North Pole, marking a new era in Arctic exploration and military capability.

Throughout the 20th century, Arctic exploration continued to evolve, with a growing emphasis on scientific research and environmental conservation. The establishment of the International Geophysical Year (1957-1958) saw a coordinated global effort to study the Arctic and its role in the Earth's climate system. Scientists from multiple countries conducted research on Arctic ice, ocean currents, and atmospheric conditions, laying the foundation for modern climate science. In the decades that followed, the Arctic became a focal point for research on climate change, as scientists recognized that the region was particularly sensitive to rising global temperatures.

In recent years, Arctic exploration has taken on new dimensions as the impacts of climate change have become increasingly apparent. The Arctic is warming at a rate twice as fast as the global average, leading to the rapid melting of sea ice, glaciers, and permafrost. As a result, previously inaccessible areas of the Arctic are becoming more open to human activity, including shipping, resource extraction, and tourism. The shrinking of Arctic sea ice has also renewed interest in the Northwest Passage, which is now navigable for longer periods each year due to the reduction in ice cover.

However, the opening of the Arctic presents significant environmental and geopolitical challenges. The Arctic is home to fragile ecosystems that are already under threat from climate change, and increased human activity could further disrupt wildlife populations and degrade the environment. In addition, the Arctic's vast reserves of oil, natural gas, and minerals have sparked competition among Arctic nations, including the United States, Canada, Russia, Norway, and Denmark, all of which have territorial claims in the region. The potential for resource conflicts and environmental damage has led to calls for greater international cooperation and regulation to protect the Arctic's unique and vulnerable environment.

In conclusion, the history of Arctic exploration is a rich and complex story that reflects humanity's enduring fascination with the unknown and the extremes of the natural world. From the earliest indigenous inhabitants to the daring European explorers who sought new trade routes and the modern scientists studying the impacts of climate change, the Arctic has always been a place of both challenge and discovery. While many explorers paid a high price for their ambitions, their efforts have greatly expanded our knowledge of the Arctic and its importance to the planet's climate and ecosystems. As the Arctic continues to change in the face of global warming, the lessons learned from centuries of exploration will be more important than ever in guiding efforts to protect this unique and fragile region for future generations.

Chapter 12: Whales of the Arctic Waters

Whales are among the most majestic and iconic creatures that inhabit the Arctic waters, and their presence in this remote and often harsh environment has fascinated scientists, explorers, and indigenous peoples for centuries. The Arctic is home to several species of whales, each uniquely adapted to survive in the cold, icy waters of the region. These whales play a critical role in the Arctic marine ecosystem, acting as top predators and helping to maintain the balance of the food web. The history, biology, and behavior of these Arctic whales, as well as their interactions with humans, provide a fascinating window into the complex and interconnected world of Arctic wildlife. Understanding the lives of these whales is also vital for their conservation, as they face numerous threats from climate change, industrial activity, and hunting.

The Arctic Ocean and surrounding seas are home to three main species of whales that are known to reside there year-round: the bowhead whale, the beluga whale, and the narwhal. Additionally, several other whale species, such as the gray whale and the humpback whale, migrate to the Arctic during the summer months to take advantage of the region's rich feeding grounds. Each of these species has evolved remarkable adaptations that allow them to thrive in the frigid and often ice-covered waters of the Arctic.

The bowhead whale (*Balaena mysticetus*) is one of the most iconic species of the Arctic. This massive baleen whale, which can grow up to 60 feet in length and weigh as much as 100 tons, is perfectly suited to life in the icy waters of the Arctic. Bowhead whales are named for their distinctive, bow-shaped skulls, which are incredibly thick and strong. This adaptation allows them to break through sea ice that can be over a foot thick, enabling them to breathe in ice-covered areas where other whales might be unable to survive. Bowheads have the thickest blubber of any whale species, with layers up to 20 inches thick, providing essential insulation against the extreme cold.

Bowhead whales are also known for their long lifespan, with some individuals believed to live over 200 years, making them among the longest-lived mammals on Earth. This remarkable longevity is a testament to their ability to survive in one of the planet's harshest environments. Bowheads are baleen whales, meaning they feed by filtering small organisms, such as zooplankton and krill, through baleen plates in their mouths. In the Arctic, they feed primarily on copepods and other tiny marine organisms that are abundant in the nutrient-rich waters of the region.

Beluga whales (*Delphinapterus leucas*), often referred to as "canaries of the sea" due to their high-pitched vocalizations, are another species that calls the Arctic home. These small, white whales are highly social and live in pods, often migrating between summer and winter habitats in search of food and suitable calving grounds. Belugas are well adapted to the Arctic environment, with a layer of blubber that provides insulation and buoyancy. Unlike many other whale species, belugas do not have dorsal fins, which helps them navigate under sea ice without injury. Their flexible necks allow them to turn their heads in different directions, a useful adaptation for navigating through narrow ice channels or searching for prey in the water.

Belugas are particularly well known for their complex vocalizations, which include a wide range of clicks, whistles, and chirps. These sounds are used for communication within pods and for echolocation, a form of biological sonar that helps them locate prey and navigate in the often murky waters of the Arctic. Belugas are opportunistic feeders, preying on a variety of fish, squid, and crustaceans. During the summer months, they often move into shallow, warmer coastal waters and river estuaries, where they molt their skin and feed on abundant fish populations.

The narwhal (*Monodon monoceros*), sometimes called the "unicorn of the sea," is one of the most mysterious and unique whales of the Arctic. Narwhals are medium-sized whales that are closely related to belugas. They are best known for the long, spiral tusk that protrudes from the heads of males, which can grow up to 10 feet long. This tusk is actually an elongated tooth, and while its exact function remains something of a mystery, scientists believe it may play a role in mating displays or social dominance. Narwhals are deep divers, capable of reaching depths of up to 5,000 feet in search of food, primarily fish like Arctic cod and Greenland halibut.

Narwhals, like belugas, are highly vocal and use echolocation to navigate and hunt in the dark waters of the Arctic. They live in small groups, or pods, and are known for their seasonal migrations between summer feeding grounds in coastal waters and wintering areas in deeper, ice-covered seas. Narwhals are highly adapted to life in icy environments, with thick layers of blubber for insulation and the ability to travel long distances under ice in search of breathing holes.

In addition to these resident species, several other whale species migrate to the Arctic during the summer months. Gray whales (*Eschrichtius robustus*) and humpback whales (*Megaptera novaeangliae*) are two of the most notable seasonal visitors. Gray whales undertake one of the longest migrations of any mammal, traveling from their breeding grounds in the warm waters off Mexico to the rich feeding grounds of the Bering, Chukchi, and Beaufort Seas in the Arctic. There, they feed on benthic organisms, such as amphipods, by filtering sediment from the ocean floor through their baleen plates.

Humpback whales are also known for their long migrations, traveling from tropical breeding areas to the cold, food-rich waters of the Arctic. These whales are famous for their acrobatic breaches and complex songs, which are believed to play a role in mating behavior. In the Arctic, humpbacks feed primarily on krill and small fish, using a technique known as bubble-net feeding to corral and capture large amounts of prey.

The whales of the Arctic are not only fascinating in their biology and behavior, but they also play a critical role in the marine ecosystem.

As top predators, whales help regulate the populations of their prey, ensuring the health and balance of the Arctic food web. Additionally, whales contribute to the cycling of nutrients in the ocean through their feeding and defecation, which can stimulate the growth of phytoplankton and other marine organisms.

Whales have also played a significant role in the cultures of the indigenous peoples of the Arctic, such as the Inuit, Chukchi, and Sami. For thousands of years, these communities have relied on whales for food, oil, and materials for clothing and tools. Whale hunting, or whaling, has been an important cultural and subsistence activity, with intricate traditions and knowledge surrounding the hunting, processing, and use of whales. Indigenous whaling practices are highly sustainable, with hunters taking only what is needed for their communities and using nearly every part of the whale. However, the arrival of European and American whalers in the Arctic in the 18th and 19th centuries had a devastating impact on whale populations.

Commercial whaling in the Arctic reached its peak during the 19th century, as whalers sought the valuable blubber, baleen, and oil that could be extracted from whales. Bowhead whales, in particular, were heavily targeted, and their populations were severely depleted as a result. The industrial whaling fleets of Europe and North America hunted whales on an unsustainable scale, leading to the near-extinction of several species. By the early 20th century, many Arctic whale populations had been reduced to a fraction of their original numbers.

The decline of commercial whaling in the mid-20th century, combined with the introduction of international regulations, such as the 1982 moratorium on commercial whaling by the International Whaling Commission (IWC), has allowed some Arctic whale populations to begin recovering. However, whales in the Arctic continue to face significant threats, particularly from climate change. The warming of the Arctic is leading to a loss of sea ice, which is a crucial habitat for many whale species. The reduction of ice cover is also opening up new shipping routes and increasing industrial activity in the Arctic, leading to concerns about pollution, noise disturbance, and collisions with ships.

The melting of sea ice is also affecting the availability of prey for whales, particularly species like narwhals and bowheads that rely on ice-associated organisms. As the Arctic environment changes, whales may be forced to adapt to new conditions or face population declines. Additionally, the warming of Arctic waters is causing shifts in the distribution of fish and other prey species, which could have cascading effects on the entire marine food web.

Conservation efforts are underway to protect Arctic whales and their habitats. Marine protected areas, such as the Arctic National Wildlife Refuge and Canada's Lancaster Sound National Marine Conservation Area, provide important refuges for whales and other marine life. International cooperation is also critical, as many whale species migrate across national boundaries and are affected by activities in multiple countries.

In conclusion, the whales of the Arctic waters are extraordinary creatures, each uniquely adapted to life in one of the most challenging environments on Earth. From the massive bowhead whale, with its remarkable longevity and ice-breaking abilities, to the elusive and mysterious narwhal, these whales are integral to the Arctic ecosystem and hold a special place in the culture and history of the region's indigenous peoples. However, they face numerous threats from climate change, industrial activity, and historical overhunting. The future of Arctic whales will depend on the collective efforts of nations, scientists, and conservationists to protect their habitats and ensure their survival in a rapidly changing world.

Chapter 13: The Role of the Arctic Council

The Arctic Council is one of the most important intergovernmental organizations dedicated to promoting cooperation, coordination, and interaction among Arctic states and indigenous communities. Established in 1996, the Council plays a critical role in addressing a wide range of issues specific to the Arctic region, including environmental protection, sustainable development, climate change, scientific research, and the well-being of the indigenous peoples who live there. The Arctic Council is unique in its structure and scope, as it is composed of both Arctic states and Permanent Participants, which represent indigenous groups, making it a platform that emphasizes inclusivity and the interests of those most directly affected by changes in the Arctic. The Council's work has grown in prominence over the years, as the Arctic increasingly becomes a focal point of global attention due to the region's vast natural resources, its strategic geopolitical importance, and the accelerating impacts of climate change.

The Arctic Council was formally established by the Ottawa Declaration on September 19, 1996, by the eight Arctic states: Canada, Denmark (including Greenland and the Faroe Islands), Finland, Iceland, Norway, Sweden, Russia, and the United States. These states make up the core members of the Council, and they share a common interest in addressing the unique challenges and opportunities of the Arctic region. The Ottawa Declaration also established the participation of indigenous groups, referred to as Permanent Participants, giving them a formal voice in decision-making processes. The Permanent Participants include six organizations: the Inuit Circumpolar Council (representing Inuit from Alaska, Canada, Greenland, and Russia), the Saami Council (representing the Sami people of Finland, Norway, Russia, and Sweden), the Russian Association of Indigenous Peoples of the North (RAIPON), the Aleut International Association, the Gwich'in Council International, and the Arctic Athabaskan Council. This structure makes the Arctic Council distinctive among intergovernmental organizations, as it provides indigenous peoples with a significant role in shaping policies that directly affect their communities and the lands they have traditionally inhabited.

One of the main roles of the Arctic Council is to serve as a forum for dialogue and cooperation on issues related to environmental protection and sustainable development. The Arctic is a region of immense ecological importance, home to diverse wildlife, unique ecosystems, and vital natural resources. However, it is also one of the regions most vulnerable to the impacts of climate change, with rising temperatures, melting sea ice, thawing permafrost, and shifting ecosystems all posing serious threats to both the environment and the people who live there. The Council works to foster collaboration on scientific research and environmental monitoring, enabling Arctic states to share data, knowledge, and best practices for managing these challenges. One of its core working groups, the Arctic Monitoring and Assessment Programme (AMAP), plays a critical role in monitoring environmental conditions in the Arctic, assessing the impacts of climate change, and providing scientific advice to governments and policymakers. AMAP has been instrumental in documenting the dramatic changes occurring in the Arctic, including the rapid loss of sea ice, rising temperatures, and the increasing prevalence of extreme weather events.

The Arctic Council also focuses on issues related to sustainable development, seeking to balance the need for economic growth and resource development with environmental protection and the preservation of indigenous cultures and traditions. The Arctic is rich in natural resources, including oil, gas, minerals, and fish, and these resources have attracted increasing attention from governments and industries around the world. However, resource extraction in the Arctic presents significant risks, including environmental degradation, habitat destruction, and the potential for oil spills or other accidents that could have catastrophic consequences for the fragile Arctic ecosystem. The Council promotes responsible resource management and encourages Arctic states to adopt best practices for minimizing the environmental and social impacts of resource development. One of its key working groups, the Sustainable Development Working Group (SDWG), focuses on promoting economic and social development in the Arctic while ensuring that the needs and rights of indigenous peoples are respected and that the environment is protected for future generations.

Another important function of the Arctic Council is to facilitate cooperation on scientific research and knowledge sharing. The Arctic is a region of great scientific interest, offering valuable insights into a wide range of fields, from climate science and oceanography to geology and biology. The Council provides a platform for Arctic states and indigenous communities to collaborate on scientific research, share data and findings, and coordinate efforts to address common challenges. One of its most significant initiatives in this area is the Arctic Council's Arctic Science Cooperation Agreement, which was signed by all eight Arctic states in 2017. This agreement aims to facilitate international cooperation on scientific research in the Arctic by simplifying the process of conducting research across national borders, improving access to research infrastructure and data, and encouraging collaboration among scientists from different countries.

The Arctic Council has also played a critical role in addressing the impacts of climate change, which poses perhaps the most pressing and far-reaching challenge facing the Arctic region today. The Arctic is warming at more than twice the rate of the global average, a phenomenon known as Arctic amplification, and the effects of this warming are profound. Sea ice is disappearing at an alarming rate, threatening the habitats of polar bears, seals, and other wildlife, while also opening up new shipping routes and opportunities for resource extraction. Permafrost is thawing, releasing large amounts of carbon dioxide and methane into the atmosphere and contributing to global warming. Coastal communities are facing increased risks from erosion, storm surges, and rising sea levels. The Arctic Council has been at the forefront of efforts to address these challenges, working to raise awareness of the impacts of climate change, promote adaptation and mitigation strategies, and coordinate international action.

One of the Council's most notable achievements in the area of climate change was its role in the negotiation of the Agreement on Enhancing International Arctic Scientific Cooperation, which was signed in 2017. This agreement was a major milestone in fostering greater collaboration among Arctic states on climate research and monitoring, and it has helped to advance our understanding of how climate change is affecting the Arctic and what can be done to mitigate its impacts. The Council has also been instrumental in addressing issues related to black carbon and methane emissions, which are potent greenhouse gases that contribute to Arctic warming. In 2015, the Arctic Council adopted a framework for action on black carbon and methane, which encourages Arctic states to reduce their emissions of these pollutants and improve air quality in the region.

The Arctic Council's work is not limited to environmental and scientific issues; it also plays a vital role in promoting the well-being and rights of the indigenous peoples of the Arctic. Indigenous communities have lived in the Arctic for thousands of years, developing deep knowledge of the land, sea, and ice, as well as unique cultural practices and traditions. However, these communities are among the most vulnerable to the impacts of climate change and other environmental pressures, such as industrial development, pollution, and habitat loss. The Arctic Council provides a platform for indigenous groups to have a voice in decisions that affect their lands and livelihoods, ensuring that their perspectives are heard and respected. The Permanent Participants play a key role in shaping the Council's agenda and advocating for the rights and interests of indigenous peoples. The Council's work in this area includes initiatives to support indigenous language preservation, health and well-being, education, and sustainable livelihoods.

In recent years, the Arctic Council has also become an important forum for addressing geopolitical and security concerns in the Arctic. As the Arctic becomes more accessible due to the loss of sea ice, new opportunities for shipping, resource extraction, and military activity are emerging, raising concerns about potential conflicts and competition among Arctic states. The Council provides a platform for dialogue and cooperation on these issues, helping to reduce tensions and promote peaceful cooperation in the region. Although the Council's mandate explicitly excludes military security issues, it plays an important role in promoting stability and cooperation through initiatives related to search and rescue, pollution prevention, and maritime safety.

The Arctic Council's emphasis on collaboration, consensus, and diplomacy has allowed it to remain a successful and influential organization despite the growing geopolitical and economic interest in the Arctic. One of its most significant achievements in this regard was the negotiation of the 2011 Agreement on Cooperation on Aeronautical and Maritime Search and Rescue in the Arctic, which was the first legally binding agreement negotiated under the auspices of the Arctic Council. This agreement established a framework for cooperation among Arctic states in responding to emergencies and disasters in the Arctic, a region where harsh conditions and vast distances make search and rescue operations particularly challenging.

Another important agreement facilitated by the Arctic Council is the 2013 Agreement on Cooperation on Marine Oil Pollution Preparedness and Response in the Arctic. This agreement aims to enhance cooperation among Arctic states in preventing and responding to oil spills in the Arctic, where the risks of oil spills are heightened by the region's extreme weather, ice cover, and fragile ecosystems. The agreement underscores the importance of international collaboration in protecting the Arctic environment from the potentially devastating consequences of industrial accidents.

The Arctic Council has also played a role in fostering cooperation on fisheries management in the region. As climate change alters the distribution of fish stocks in the Arctic, there is growing interest in developing commercial fisheries in previously inaccessible areas. To address this issue, the Arctic Council helped pave the way for the 2018 Agreement to Prevent Unregulated High Seas Fisheries in the Central Arctic Ocean. This agreement, signed by the eight Arctic states as well as China, Japan, South Korea, and the European Union, establishes a moratorium on commercial fishing in the Central Arctic Ocean until more is known about the health and sustainability of fish stocks in the region. The agreement reflects the Council's commitment to precautionary approaches to resource management and its recognition of the need for international cooperation to protect Arctic ecosystems.

In conclusion, the Arctic Council plays a vital and multifaceted role in addressing the unique challenges and opportunities of the Arctic region. Through its focus on environmental protection, sustainable development, scientific research, indigenous rights, and international cooperation, the Council has become a leading forum for addressing the complex and interconnected issues facing the Arctic. As the region continues to undergo rapid changes due to climate change and increased human activity, the Arctic Council's work will only become more important in shaping the future of the Arctic and ensuring that it remains a place of peace, stability, and sustainability. The Council's collaborative approach, which brings together governments, indigenous peoples, scientists, and stakeholders from around the world, is a model for how the international community can work together to address the pressing challenges of our time.

Chapter 14: Unique Arctic Plants

The Arctic region, often thought of as a barren, icy wilderness, is home to a surprising variety of plant life. Despite the extreme conditions, including freezing temperatures, strong winds, permafrost, and a short growing season, many unique plants have adapted to survive and even thrive in the harsh Arctic environment. These plants are critical to the Arctic ecosystem, providing food and shelter for wildlife, helping to stabilize the soil, and playing a vital role in the delicate balance of the tundra and other Arctic landscapes. The adaptations that allow Arctic plants to survive in such extreme conditions are remarkable, and studying them not only enhances our understanding of botany and ecology but also offers valuable insights into how life can persist in some of the most inhospitable environments on Earth.

Arctic plants are part of a larger ecosystem called the tundra, a treeless biome that extends across the northern parts of Alaska, Canada, Russia, Greenland, and Scandinavia. The tundra is characterized by its cold, windy climate, short growing seasons, and permafrost—soil that remains frozen year-round. These factors present numerous challenges to plant life, but over millennia, Arctic plants have developed a range of adaptations to overcome these challenges. Many of these adaptations center around their ability to maximize growth and reproduction during the brief Arctic summer when the sun shines nearly 24 hours a day, but temperatures still remain cool, and the growing season lasts only about 50 to 60 days.

One of the most obvious challenges for Arctic plants is the cold. Even during the summer, temperatures can drop below freezing, and frost can occur at any time. To cope with the cold, many Arctic plants are low-growing and form dense mats or cushions that hug the ground. This growth habit not only helps to protect them from the cold winds but also allows them to absorb heat from the sun more effectively. By growing close to the ground, these plants take advantage of the slightly warmer temperatures near the surface of the soil, which can be a few degrees higher than the air temperature. Cushion plants, such as moss campion (*Silene acaulis*) and Arctic dryad (*Dryas octopetala*), are classic examples of this growth form. They form compact, dome-shaped mats that trap heat and reduce water loss through evaporation.

In addition to their low-growing habit, many Arctic plants have developed specialized leaves to cope with the cold and dry conditions. Some plants, such as Arctic willows (*Salix arctica*), have leaves that are covered in tiny hairs, which help to trap heat and protect the plant from wind and cold. These hairs also help to reduce water loss by creating a microenvironment of still air around the leaf surface. Other plants, like the Arctic poppy (*Papaver radicatum*), have leaves that are dark in color, which helps them absorb more heat from the sun. This adaptation is particularly important in the Arctic, where even a few degrees of warmth can make a significant difference in a plant's ability to grow and reproduce.

Water is another limiting factor for plant life in the Arctic. Although the tundra is often thought of as a cold desert, it can be quite wet in the summer when the snow and ice melt. However, the permafrost beneath the soil prevents water from draining away, and the shallow, waterlogged soil can become a challenge for plant roots. To deal with this, many Arctic plants have shallow root systems that allow them to take advantage of the water that is available at the surface without having to penetrate the frozen ground below. Some plants, like cotton grass (*Eriophorum angustifolium*), are adapted to grow in waterlogged soils and are commonly found in wet tundra areas and Arctic wetlands.

One of the most fascinating aspects of Arctic plant life is the way these plants have adapted to the extreme seasonal changes in daylight. During the summer, the Arctic experiences nearly 24 hours of sunlight, while in the winter, the region is plunged into darkness for months. This dramatic variation in light availability presents a unique challenge for plant growth and reproduction. Arctic plants have evolved to take full advantage of the short but intense Arctic summer. Many species begin growing as soon as the snow melts, and they flower and set seed very quickly to ensure they complete their life cycle before the short growing season ends. Some species, such as the Arctic poppy and the purple saxifrage (*Saxifraga oppositifolia*), can bloom just days after the snow melts, often while patches of snow are still visible on the ground.

In addition to their rapid life cycles, many Arctic plants have developed ways to maximize the amount of sunlight they receive. The Arctic poppy, for example, has flowers that track the sun's movement across the sky, a behavior known as heliotropism. By following the sun, the flowers can maintain a warmer temperature in their centers, which helps attract pollinators and speeds up seed development. Other plants, like the snow buttercup (*Ranunculus nivalis*), have bowl-shaped flowers that act as solar collectors, concentrating sunlight onto the reproductive organs of the flower to keep them warm.

Pollination can be a challenge in the Arctic, where the cold temperatures and short growing season limit the activity of pollinators such as bees and butterflies. To overcome this, some Arctic plants have developed strategies to ensure successful reproduction even in the absence of regular pollinators. Many Arctic plants are capable of self-pollination, which allows them to produce seeds without relying on insects to transfer pollen from one flower to another. This adaptation is particularly useful in the Arctic, where pollinators may be scarce or inactive due to the cold weather. Other plants, like the Arctic willow, produce catkins (dense clusters of flowers) that are wind-pollinated, reducing their dependence on insect pollinators.

One of the most iconic and widespread Arctic plants is the Arctic moss (*Calliergon giganteum*), a type of bryophyte that thrives in the cold, wet conditions of the tundra. Mosses are well-suited to the Arctic because they do not have roots, instead absorbing water and nutrients directly through their leaves. This allows them to grow in areas where other plants cannot, such as on rocks, in shallow soils, or in waterlogged areas. Mosses play a crucial role in the Arctic ecosystem by helping to stabilize the soil, retain moisture, and provide habitat for small animals and microorganisms. In addition, mosses are highly resilient to freezing temperatures and can remain dormant during the winter, resuming growth as soon as conditions improve in the spring.

Lichens are another important group of organisms in the Arctic, and they are often mistaken for plants, though they are actually symbiotic associations between fungi and algae or cyanobacteria. Lichens are incredibly hardy and can survive in some of the most extreme environments on Earth, including the cold, dry conditions of the Arctic. They are particularly important in the Arctic tundra, where they are a major food source for caribou and reindeer during the winter months when other vegetation is scarce. Lichens grow very slowly but can live for hundreds or even thousands of years, making them some of the longest-living organisms in the Arctic.

The importance of Arctic plants to the region's wildlife cannot be overstated. Many Arctic animals, including caribou, musk oxen, and Arctic hares, rely on tundra vegetation for food. In the summer, the lush growth of grasses, sedges, and flowering plants provides essential nourishment for herbivores, which in turn support predators like wolves, foxes, and birds of prey. The berries produced by plants such as crowberry (*Empetrum nigrum*) and cloudberry (*Rubus chamaemorus*) are an important food source for birds, small mammals, and even bears. In winter, when most plants are dormant, hardy species like willows and lichens provide sustenance for animals adapted to the cold.

Despite their remarkable resilience, Arctic plants are facing increasing threats from climate change. As temperatures rise and permafrost thaws, the delicate balance of the Arctic ecosystem is being disrupted. Warmer temperatures are allowing shrubs and other woody plants to encroach on areas that were once dominated by low-growing tundra vegetation. This "greening" of the Arctic could have significant implications for the region's wildlife, as it may alter habitat availability and food sources. Additionally, the melting of permafrost could lead to changes in soil stability and hydrology, further affecting plant communities. Many Arctic plants are highly specialized for the cold, short growing season, and rapid changes in temperature and moisture levels could challenge their ability to survive.

In some cases, the effects of climate change are already becoming evident. For example, research has shown that Arctic plants are flowering earlier in response to warming temperatures, which could disrupt the timing of important ecological interactions, such as the availability of food for pollinators or herbivores. Earlier snowmelt and longer growing seasons may benefit some species, but others may struggle to adapt to the rapidly changing conditions.

Conservation efforts are increasingly focused on protecting Arctic ecosystems, including the unique and fragile plant life that forms the foundation of these ecosystems. Protecting the Arctic from industrial development, pollution, and the impacts of climate change is critical to ensuring the survival of these plants and the wildlife that depends on them. Researchers are also studying Arctic plants to better understand their adaptations to extreme conditions, which could have applications in agriculture and other fields as the global climate continues to change.

In conclusion, the unique plants of the Arctic are a testament to the incredible resilience and adaptability of life in one of the harshest environments on Earth. From low-growing cushion plants and hardy mosses to lichens and berry-producing shrubs, Arctic vegetation plays a vital role in the region's ecosystems, supporting wildlife, stabilizing the soil, and contributing to the overall health of the tundra. However, these plants are increasingly threatened by climate change and human activity, and their future depends on our ability to protect and conserve the fragile Arctic environment. The study of Arctic plants not only enriches our understanding of biology and ecology but also offers valuable lessons in adaptation, survival, and the interconnectedness of life on Earth.

81

Chapter 15: Aurora Borealis Science

The Aurora Borealis, commonly known as the Northern Lights, is one of the most spectacular natural phenomena visible in the skies of the Arctic and high-latitude regions. This breathtaking display of colorful lights—ranging from shades of green, pink, purple, red, and blue—dances across the night sky in vivid curtains, arcs, and streaks. The science behind this magnificent phenomenon is deeply rooted in the interactions between the Earth's magnetic field, the sun's solar winds, and the atmosphere. Understanding the Aurora Borealis requires a grasp of space weather, magnetism, and the behavior of charged particles. Although ancient cultures attributed the Northern Lights to supernatural forces or mythological stories, modern science has explained the aurora in terms of physics and astronomy, giving us insight into how energy from the sun interacts with the Earth's magnetic shield to produce such stunning visual effects.

At its core, the Aurora Borealis is caused by the interaction of solar wind particles with the Earth's magnetosphere and atmosphere. Solar winds, which are streams of charged particles (mainly electrons and protons) emitted by the sun, constantly flow outward into space. These winds are carried by the solar corona, the sun's outer atmosphere, which is extremely hot and constantly in motion. While the sun emits these particles all the time, the intensity of the solar wind fluctuates depending on solar activity, such as solar flares and coronal mass ejections. When the solar wind reaches Earth, it collides with the planet's magnetic field, which acts as a shield, protecting the surface from the direct impact of these charged particles.

The Earth's magnetic field is not uniform; it is shaped like a large, invisible bubble that extends far into space. This magnetic field is stronger at the poles, forming two regions known as the magnetospheric polar caps, where the magnetic lines of force converge. When solar wind particles hit this magnetic field, they are funneled toward the polar regions because the field lines there are open, allowing the particles to penetrate deeper into the Earth's atmosphere. This is why auroras are most commonly seen near the poles, in places like the Arctic Circle and the Southern Hemisphere. In the Northern Hemisphere, the phenomenon is called the Aurora Borealis, and in the Southern Hemisphere, it is called the Aurora Australis.

The solar wind particles that reach the Earth's magnetic field are composed of electrons and protons, which are electrically charged. As these particles spiral along the Earth's magnetic field lines and are funneled toward the polar regions, they eventually enter the Earth's atmosphere. Here, they collide with gas molecules, primarily oxygen and nitrogen, in the thermosphere, which is located about 80 to 500 kilometers above the Earth's surface. These collisions transfer energy to the gas molecules, exciting them to higher energy states. When these excited molecules return to their normal energy state, they release photons, or light particles, creating the beautiful glowing patterns that we observe as the aurora.

The colors of the Aurora Borealis are determined by the type of gas molecules involved in the collisions, the altitude at which the collisions occur, and the energy of the incoming particles. The most common auroral color is green, which is produced by oxygen molecules that are excited at altitudes of about 100 to 300 kilometers above the Earth's surface. Green auroras are by far the most frequently observed because oxygen is abundant in the atmosphere, and the energy level required to excite oxygen at these altitudes is relatively low. However, auroras can also appear in other colors, depending on the specific conditions in the atmosphere.

For instance, red auroras, though rarer, occur when high-energy electrons collide with oxygen atoms at altitudes above 300 kilometers. At these higher altitudes, the lower density of the atmosphere allows oxygen to emit red light before the energy dissipates. Nitrogen molecules also contribute to the auroral colors, with ionized nitrogen producing blue or purplish hues, and molecular nitrogen resulting in shades of violet and pink. These colors are typically observed at the edges of the auroral displays, where nitrogen is more abundant.

In addition to the striking colors, the Aurora Borealis is known for its dynamic and ever-changing shapes and movements. Auroras often appear as arcs, curtains, or bands that stretch across the sky, and they can pulsate, flicker, or undulate in response to fluctuations in the solar wind and the Earth's magnetic field. The complex shapes and movements of the aurora are influenced by the interactions between the solar wind and the magnetosphere, with stronger solar wind activity resulting in more intense and dramatic displays. During periods of heightened solar activity, such as solar storms or geomagnetic storms, auroras can become particularly vibrant and may even be visible at lower latitudes, far beyond the typical Arctic regions.

Solar storms, or geomagnetic storms, occur when the sun experiences an intense burst of solar activity, such as a solar flare or a coronal mass ejection (CME). These events release vast amounts of energy and charged particles into space, increasing the intensity of the solar wind. When a CME reaches Earth, it can compress the magnetosphere and cause a surge of charged particles to enter the atmosphere, leading to especially bright and widespread auroras. Geomagnetic storms can have significant effects on the Earth's magnetic field, sometimes disrupting communication systems, power grids, and satellite operations. However, they also create some of the most awe-inspiring auroral displays, with colors and shapes that can stretch across vast areas of the sky.

The science of the Aurora Borealis has been a subject of fascination for centuries. Early explanations for the phenomenon were often rooted in mythology and folklore, with various cultures interpreting the lights as spiritual or supernatural events. The Vikings, for example, believed that the Northern Lights were reflections from the shields and armor of the Valkyries, warrior maidens who carried fallen soldiers to

Valhalla. In Inuit culture, the auroras were thought to be the spirits of ancestors playing games in the sky, while in other indigenous traditions, they were seen as messages from the gods or as omens of significant events.

The first scientific attempts to explain the Northern Lights began in the 17th century, when the astronomer Galileo Galilei coined the term "Aurora Borealis," combining the name of the Roman goddess of dawn, Aurora, with the Greek name for the north wind, Boreas. Galileo mistakenly believed that the auroras were caused by sunlight reflecting off the Earth's atmosphere, but his observations helped to spark further scientific inquiry into the phenomenon.

In the 18th century, the British astronomer Edmond Halley proposed that the auroras were related to the Earth's magnetic field, a theory that laid the groundwork for modern understanding of the phenomenon. Halley suggested that the auroras were caused by particles from the sun interacting with the Earth's magnetic field, an idea that was later confirmed through advances in physics and space science. In the 20th century, scientists such as Kristian Birkeland and Carl Stormer made significant contributions to the study of the auroras, using balloons, rockets, and satellite technology to study the behavior of charged particles in the Earth's magnetosphere.

One of the most important discoveries in auroral science came with the development of the theory of solar wind in the mid-20th century. Scientists realized that the sun constantly emits a stream of charged particles, which interact with the Earth's magnetic field to produce the auroras. This understanding was further refined with the advent of space exploration, which allowed scientists to directly observe the interactions between solar wind and the magnetosphere. Satellites and spacecraft have provided invaluable data on the solar wind, the behavior of charged particles, and the structure of the Earth's magnetic field, helping to refine our understanding of the mechanisms that produce the auroras.

Today, scientists continue to study the Aurora Borealis using a variety of tools and techniques, including ground-based observatories, satellite missions, and computer models. One of the key areas of research is the relationship between solar activity and auroral displays, particularly during periods of intense solar storms. Understanding how solar wind interacts with the Earth's magnetosphere is crucial not only for predicting auroras but also for protecting satellites, power grids, and communication systems from the effects of space weather.

Another area of interest is the study of auroral sounds, which have been reported by observers for centuries. Some people claim to hear faint crackling or rustling sounds during auroral displays, though these reports are rare and not well understood. Scientists have been investigating whether these sounds are caused by electrical discharges in the atmosphere, low-frequency radio waves, or other mechanisms, but definitive evidence remains elusive.

The Aurora Borealis also plays a significant role in indigenous cultures and traditional knowledge systems in the Arctic. Many indigenous peoples, including the Sami, Inuit, and First Nations, have long observed and interpreted the auroras as part of their cultural heritage. In some traditions, the Northern Lights are believed to have spiritual significance, representing ancestors or celestial beings. In others, they are viewed as omens or messages from the natural world. For many Arctic communities, the auroras are an integral part of the landscape, reflecting the deep connection between the environment and human life.

In recent years, the auroras have also become a major attraction for tourists and travelers, with people from around the world flocking to Arctic regions to witness the spectacle. Northern Norway, Finland, Canada, Iceland, and Alaska are popular destinations for aurora-watching, with specialized tours and lodges offering opportunities to experience the lights firsthand. The rise of aurora tourism has brought economic benefits to many Arctic communities, but it has also raised concerns about environmental impacts and the need to preserve the delicate Arctic ecosystems that support the phenomenon.

In conclusion, the Aurora Borealis, or Northern Lights, is a mesmerizing natural phenomenon that combines the forces of space weather, magnetism, and atmospheric science to produce one of the most beautiful displays on Earth. The vivid colors and dynamic movements of the auroras are the result of complex interactions between solar wind particles, the Earth's magnetic field, and the gases in the atmosphere. While scientists have made great strides in understanding the auroras, there is still much to learn about the precise mechanisms that drive this phenomenon and its broader implications for space weather and the Earth's magnetic environment. As we continue to study and marvel at the Aurora Borealis, we are reminded of the beauty and complexity of the natural world and the ways in which our planet is connected to the vast forces of the cosmos.

Chapter 16: The Life of Walruses

Walruses are among the most iconic and fascinating marine mammals of the Arctic. Known for their large, tusked appearance and their bulky, wrinkled bodies, walruses are uniquely adapted to life in one of the most challenging environments on Earth. These massive creatures have evolved a suite of physical and behavioral traits that enable them to thrive in the icy waters of the Arctic Ocean, where they live alongside seals, polar bears, and other species. Despite their slow-moving, lumbering appearance on land, walruses are graceful swimmers and powerful divers, capable of withstanding freezing temperatures and enduring long periods in the water as they hunt for food. Understanding the life of walruses reveals not only the intricacies of their biology and ecology but also the broader dynamics of the Arctic ecosystem and the ways in which these animals have been deeply intertwined with the cultures and economies of indigenous peoples for millennia.

Walruses belong to the pinniped family, which also includes seals and sea lions, but they are distinguished by several key features, most notably their long, curved tusks. These tusks, which are actually elongated canine teeth, can grow up to 3 feet (about 1 meter) in length and serve a variety of functions in the walrus's life. Both male and female walruses have tusks, although males typically have larger and more robust ones. The tusks are used for a variety of purposes, including helping the walrus haul itself out of the water onto ice floes, fighting with other walruses for dominance, and defending against predators like polar bears and orcas. The tusks are also a sign of social status within walrus herds, with larger, more impressive tusks indicating a stronger or more dominant individual.

In addition to their tusks, walruses are known for their thick layer of blubber, which can be up to 6 inches (15 centimeters) thick. This blubber serves as an essential insulator, helping walruses maintain their body heat in the frigid waters of the Arctic, where water temperatures can be just above freezing. The blubber also provides a valuable energy reserve during times when food is scarce, such as in the winter when ice covers much of the walrus's feeding grounds. This fat layer, along with their large size—males can weigh up to 4,400 pounds (2,000 kilograms)—makes walruses well-suited to surviving in one of the most extreme environments on Earth.

Walruses are primarily benthic feeders, meaning that they forage on the ocean floor for their food. Their diet consists mainly of mollusks, particularly clams, which they locate using their highly sensitive whiskers, or vibrissae. These whiskers, located on the walrus's snout, are densely packed with nerve endings, allowing the walrus to detect prey in the murky, often dark waters of the Arctic. Once they have found a clam or other shellfish, walruses use their powerful suction to pull the mollusk out of its shell. Rather than using their tusks to break open the shells, as was once believed, walruses create a vacuum with their mouths, sucking the soft body of the mollusk from its shell with remarkable force.

Walruses can dive to depths of around 300 feet (90 meters) and remain submerged for up to 30 minutes while searching for food. Their ability to stay underwater for such long periods is due to several physiological adaptations, including the ability to slow their heart rate, a process known as bradycardia, which reduces oxygen consumption. Walruses also have a large volume of blood relative to their body size, which allows them to store more oxygen and circulate it efficiently to vital organs while diving. This diving capability is crucial to their survival, as it allows them to access the benthic prey that makes up the bulk of their diet.

Walruses are highly social animals, often found in large herds that can number in the thousands. These herds, or "haul-outs," typically consist of females and their calves, while males tend to form smaller groups or live more solitary lives, particularly during the breeding season. The social structure of walrus herds is complex, with individuals establishing dominance hierarchies based on size, strength, and tusk length. Males will often engage in vocalizations, posturing, and even physical combat to establish their dominance and secure mating rights with females. These behaviors are especially pronounced during the breeding season, which takes place between January and April.

During the breeding season, male walruses, known as bulls, compete for the attention of females by engaging in elaborate vocal displays both above and below the water. These displays involve a range of sounds, including bellows, clicks, and whistles, which are amplified by air sacs located in the male's throat. These air sacs also serve another important function, allowing the walrus to float easily while sleeping in the water. Males with the most impressive vocal displays and the largest tusks are more likely to attract females for mating.

Female walruses, or cows, give birth to a single calf after a gestation period of about 15 to 16 months, which includes a period of delayed implantation. This means that after mating, the fertilized egg does not immediately implant in the uterus but instead remains dormant for several months before beginning to develop. This delayed implantation ensures that the calf is born during the following spring, when conditions are more favorable for its survival. Calves are usually born on ice floes, where they can be protected from predators, and they weigh around 100 to 165 pounds (45 to 75 kilograms) at birth.

Walrus calves are highly dependent on their mothers for the first two years of their lives. They nurse on their mother's rich milk, which is high in fat and provides the energy needed for rapid growth. During this time, the mother and calf maintain a close bond, with the mother providing protection and teaching the calf important survival skills, such as how to find food and avoid predators. Calves begin to accompany their mothers on foraging trips at a young age, learning to use their whiskers to detect prey and practicing the suction-feeding technique that is essential for their diet.

The life of a walrus is deeply influenced by the seasonal rhythms of the Arctic environment, particularly the formation and melting of sea ice. Walruses rely on sea ice for much of their life cycle, using it as a platform for resting, giving birth, and nursing their young. In the summer, as the sea ice retreats, walruses follow the ice edge northward, remaining in the productive waters of the continental shelf, where food is abundant. During the winter, when sea ice expands, walruses move southward, often congregating in areas where the ice is thinner or broken, allowing them access to both the water and the ice for resting.

The dependence of walruses on sea ice makes them particularly vulnerable to the effects of climate change. As global temperatures rise, the Arctic is experiencing a dramatic loss of sea ice, which poses significant challenges for walruses. In recent years, scientists have observed an increase in the number of walruses hauling out on land instead of ice, particularly along the coasts of Alaska and Russia. These land-based haul-outs can be dangerous for walruses, especially for young calves, as they are more exposed to predators and human activity. Additionally, the long distances between haul-out sites and feeding grounds can cause exhaustion and reduce the amount of time walruses can spend foraging for food.

The loss of sea ice also affects the availability of prey. As the Arctic warms, changes in ocean temperature and circulation patterns are altering the distribution of benthic species like clams, which are a primary food source for walruses. This can force walruses to travel farther and dive deeper to find sufficient food, further increasing their energy expenditure and reducing their overall fitness. The impacts of climate change on walrus populations are still being studied, but there is growing concern that these changes could lead to a decline in walrus numbers in the coming decades.

Walruses have been an important part of the cultures and economies of Arctic indigenous peoples for thousands of years. Indigenous communities, such as the Inuit and Chukchi, have traditionally hunted walruses for their meat, blubber, and tusks, which are used for food, oil, clothing, tools, and art. Walrus hunting is deeply embedded in the cultural practices and spiritual beliefs of these peoples, and it plays a central role in their subsistence lifestyles. For many Arctic communities, the walrus is not just a source of material resources but also a symbol of resilience and adaptation to the harsh environment of the North.

In modern times, walrus hunting is regulated to ensure sustainable practices and to protect walrus populations from overharvesting. Indigenous peoples in Alaska, Canada, Greenland, and Russia are allowed to hunt walruses under traditional and subsistence hunting rights, and these hunts are carefully managed to balance the needs of local communities with the conservation of walrus populations. In some regions, walrus hunts are an important economic activity, with the sale of walrus ivory and other products providing income for indigenous families.

Despite these challenges, walruses have shown remarkable resilience in the face of changing environmental conditions. Their ability to adapt to the shifting ice and changing food availability, as well as their strong social bonds and cooperative behaviors, have allowed them to survive in the Arctic for millennia. However, the future of walruses is uncertain, as the rapid pace of climate change threatens to outstrip their ability to adapt. Conservation efforts are increasingly focused on protecting walrus habitat, reducing human impacts, and mitigating the effects of climate change to ensure that walruses continue to thrive in the Arctic for generations to come.

In conclusion, the life of walruses is a remarkable testament to the adaptability and resilience of wildlife in the Arctic. From their massive, tusked bodies to their deep-diving foraging habits, walruses are uniquely suited to life in one of the harshest environments on Earth. Their dependence on sea ice, their complex social structures, and their role in indigenous cultures highlight the intricate connections between the natural world and human societies in the Arctic. However, as climate change continues to alter the Arctic landscape, walruses face significant challenges that will require ongoing research, conservation efforts, and collaboration between scientists, policymakers, and indigenous communities to ensure their survival in a rapidly changing world.

Chapter 17: Arctic Reindeer Migration

Arctic reindeer migration is one of the most extraordinary and remarkable events in the natural world, a journey that takes place across some of the most hostile and breathtaking landscapes on Earth. These animals, also known as caribou in North America, are famous for their long-distance migrations, often covering thousands of miles across the Arctic tundra in search of food and suitable breeding grounds. Reindeer migrations are among the largest and longest in the world, with herds numbering in the hundreds of thousands, moving en masse across frozen rivers, treacherous mountain ranges, and expansive tundra. Their migration is a crucial survival strategy that allows them to cope with the extreme seasonal changes in the Arctic environment, where resources are scarce during the harsh winters, and the summers, though brief, offer a rich bounty of vegetation that is critical for their survival. Understanding the complex dynamics of Arctic reindeer migration requires not only a detailed examination of their biology and behavior but also an appreciation for the ecological, climatic, and cultural factors that influence this incredible annual journey.

Reindeer (Rangifer tarandus) are highly specialized for life in the cold, having evolved a number of physical and behavioral adaptations that allow them to endure the extreme Arctic environment. Their thick coats consist of two layers—a dense undercoat for insulation and longer, hollow guard hairs that trap air and provide additional warmth. This unique structure helps them maintain their body heat in temperatures that can drop to -50°C (-58°F) during the winter months. Additionally, their wide, concave hooves are well-suited for walking on snow and ice, as well as for digging through snow to reach the lichen and other vegetation beneath, which forms the core of their winter diet. Reindeer are the only deer species in which both males and females grow antlers, although females' antlers are typically smaller.

These antlers are used not only for defense but also for foraging, as they help scrape away snow to uncover food during the winter.

The migratory patterns of Arctic reindeer are driven primarily by the need to find food. In the summer, the tundra blooms with a variety of plants, including grasses, sedges, mosses, and lichens, which provide the reindeer with the nutrition they need to build up fat reserves for the long, cold winter ahead. During this time, reindeer travel to northern regions where the snow has melted, and the growing season is brief but intense. The lush vegetation allows them to eat almost continuously, rapidly gaining weight and building up the energy reserves that will sustain them through the lean months. In contrast, the winter months are harsh and unforgiving, with deep snow and ice covering much of the tundra, making it difficult for reindeer to access food. To survive, they must migrate southward to areas with less snow or ice, where they can continue to graze on whatever vegetation they can find, including lichens, mosses, and even the occasional willow or birch branch.

Reindeer migrations are typically seasonal, occurring twice a year—once in the spring and once in the fall. In the spring, as the Arctic begins to thaw and the snow melts, reindeer begin their northward migration toward their summer calving grounds. This journey can span hundreds or even thousands of miles, depending on the population and the region in which they live. Reindeer herds move in large groups, with tens of thousands of individuals traveling together, often forming long lines that stretch across the tundra. The exact timing of the migration depends on a variety of factors, including the length of the winter, snow and ice conditions, and the availability of food. In general, the migration begins in April or May, as the snow starts to melt and the first signs of green vegetation appear on the tundra. Calves are typically born in June, soon after the herds have reached their summer feeding grounds. The timing of the calving is crucial, as the brief Arctic summer provides a narrow window of opportunity for the calves to grow and gain strength before the return migration in the fall.

One of the most remarkable aspects of reindeer migration is the incredible distances these animals can cover. In some cases, reindeer have been recorded traveling over 3,000 miles (5,000 kilometers) in a single year, making them one of the longest-migrating terrestrial animals in the world. Their ability to undertake such long journeys is due in part to their highly efficient locomotion and energy-conserving behavior. Reindeer have a unique walking gait that allows them to move quickly and efficiently across long distances without expending excessive amounts of energy. Their large, wide hooves also play an important role in their migration, as they act like snowshoes, allowing the reindeer to traverse deep snow and soft, marshy ground without sinking.

In addition to their remarkable physical adaptations, reindeer are also highly social animals, and their migratory behavior is closely tied to their herd structure. Reindeer live in large herds, with some populations forming groups that number in the tens or even hundreds of thousands. These herds provide protection against predators, such as wolves and bears, as well as greater efficiency in finding food. Reindeer herds are led by dominant females, who play a crucial role in determining the direction and timing of the migration. During the migration, the herd moves in a coordinated manner, with individuals following closely behind the leaders, often forming long, winding lines that stretch across the tundra. This social structure helps to ensure that the herd stays together and that the young and weak individuals are protected.

The reindeer's ability to navigate across vast distances is another fascinating aspect of their migration. Studies have shown that reindeer possess an exceptional sense of direction, which is thought to be influenced by a combination of environmental cues, such as the position of the sun, the stars, and the Earth's magnetic field. In addition, reindeer are known to use olfactory and auditory signals to communicate with one another during migration, helping to maintain group cohesion and ensure that the herd remains on course.

The fall migration, which typically begins in late August or early September, is equally important for the survival of the reindeer. As the Arctic summer comes to an end and the first snow begins to fall, the reindeer must leave their northern feeding grounds and head south to their wintering areas. This migration is often more difficult than the spring migration, as the reindeer must contend with rapidly changing weather conditions, including freezing temperatures, strong winds, and deep snow. In some regions, reindeer may also have to cross rivers or other bodies of water during their migration, a task that requires both physical strength and coordination. Despite these challenges, reindeer are incredibly resilient animals, and most are able to successfully complete the journey, arriving at their wintering grounds in time to find food and shelter.

The reindeer's wintering grounds are typically located in forested areas or other regions where the snow is less deep, allowing the reindeer to dig through the snow to find food. During the winter, reindeer primarily feed on lichens, which are slow-growing organisms that thrive in the cold, dry conditions of the Arctic. These lichens, which are often referred to as "reindeer moss," provide the reindeer with the energy and nutrients they need to survive the winter. However, lichens are a relatively low-energy food source, and reindeer must eat large quantities of them to meet their nutritional needs. As a result, reindeer spend much of the winter foraging, using their hooves and antlers to scrape away the snow and uncover the lichens beneath.

Reindeer migrations are not only a natural phenomenon but also a vital aspect of the culture and livelihood of indigenous peoples in the Arctic, particularly the Sami people of Scandinavia and Russia. The Sami have been herding reindeer for thousands of years, relying on them for food, clothing, and transportation. Reindeer herding is a central part of Sami culture, and the migration of the herds is a key event in the annual cycle of Sami life. For the Sami, reindeer are more than just a source of material goods; they are also a symbol of their deep connection to the land and their traditional way of life. Sami reindeer herders often accompany their herds during migration, using their knowledge of the landscape and the behavior of the reindeer to guide the animals to their seasonal grazing areas. This relationship between the Sami and the reindeer is a powerful example of the ways in which human societies can live in harmony with the natural world, adapting to the rhythms of the environment and the needs of the animals they depend on.

The migration of reindeer is also a crucial component of the Arctic ecosystem. As they move across the tundra, reindeer play an important role in shaping the landscape and influencing the distribution of plant species. Their grazing helps to control the growth of vegetation, preventing certain plants from becoming overgrown and allowing others to thrive. In addition, reindeer provide a vital food source for predators such as wolves, bears, and wolverines, as well as for scavengers like foxes and birds of prey. The movement of reindeer herds also helps to transport nutrients across the tundra, enriching the soil and supporting the growth of new vegetation. This complex web of interactions highlights the interconnectedness of life in the Arctic and the importance of reindeer migration in maintaining the health and balance of the ecosystem.

In recent years, however, reindeer migration has been increasingly threatened by the effects of climate change. Rising temperatures, changing precipitation patterns, and the melting of sea ice are all altering the Arctic environment, with significant implications for reindeer and their migration routes. Warmer winters are leading to more frequent freeze-thaw cycles, which can create thick layers of ice on the ground, making it difficult for reindeer to access the vegetation beneath. In some areas, reindeer have been forced to travel longer distances to find food, putting additional strain on their energy reserves. At the same time, human activities such as mining, oil drilling, and infrastructure development are encroaching on traditional migration routes, further disrupting the reindeer's ability to move freely across the landscape.

The future of Arctic reindeer migration is uncertain, but there is hope that conservation efforts and sustainable management practices can help protect this vital natural phenomenon. Researchers, indigenous communities, and policymakers are working together to better understand the impacts of climate change on reindeer and to develop strategies for mitigating these effects. This includes efforts to preserve critical habitat, reduce human interference, and monitor the health of reindeer populations. The resilience and adaptability of reindeer give reason for optimism, but their continued survival will depend on our ability to address the challenges posed by a rapidly changing Arctic environment.

In conclusion, Arctic reindeer migration is a breathtaking and awe-inspiring natural event that highlights the incredible adaptability of these animals to the harsh and ever-changing conditions of the Arctic. Their migrations are not only a crucial survival strategy but also a key component of the Arctic ecosystem and the cultures of indigenous peoples. However, as climate change continues to reshape the Arctic, reindeer migration faces increasing challenges that require concerted efforts to ensure the survival of this ancient and essential phenomenon. The story of reindeer migration is one of endurance, adaptation, and the enduring connection between animals, people, and the natural world in one of the most extreme environments on Earth.

Chapter 18: The Arctic Food Web

The Arctic food web is a complex and delicate system that plays a critical role in the survival of countless species within one of the most extreme environments on Earth. In the Arctic, where temperatures plummet far below freezing for much of the year and the landscape is often covered in snow and ice, the food web is uniquely adapted to these harsh conditions. The interconnectedness of species at every level of the food chain is crucial for maintaining balance in the ecosystem, as each organism depends on another for survival. This intricate web of life extends from the smallest microscopic organisms in the Arctic Ocean to the region's apex predators, like polar bears and killer whales. The Arctic food web is an excellent example of the dynamic relationships between producers, consumers, and decomposers, and it highlights the delicate balance that exists within ecosystems, especially those subjected to extreme seasonal changes and the growing impact of climate change.

At the foundation of the Arctic food web are the primary producers—organisms that can create their own energy through the process of photosynthesis. In the Arctic, these producers are predominantly phytoplankton and sea ice algae, microscopic organisms that live in the water column or attached to the underside of sea ice. Phytoplankton, like all plant life, uses sunlight to convert carbon dioxide and nutrients into energy, releasing oxygen as a byproduct. However, in the Arctic, the availability of sunlight is highly variable due to the extreme seasonal fluctuations in daylight. During the summer months, when the sun shines for nearly 24 hours a day, phytoplankton blooms rapidly in the nutrient-rich waters, providing a massive influx of energy into the food web. This explosion of life supports a wide variety of species, from tiny zooplankton to the largest marine mammals. However, during the long, dark Arctic winter, phytoplankton growth slows significantly, and the food web must rely on stored energy or alternative sources to survive until the next burst of sunlight.

Zooplankton, which are tiny animals that drift in the ocean currents, form the next tier of the Arctic food web. These creatures feed on phytoplankton and are themselves an essential food source for many larger organisms. There are several different types of zooplankton in the Arctic, including copepods, krill, and amphipods. Copepods are small crustaceans that are particularly important in the Arctic food web because they are one of the primary consumers of phytoplankton. They are incredibly abundant in Arctic waters, especially during the summer when phytoplankton is most plentiful. Krill, another type of zooplankton, are small shrimp-like creatures that feed on phytoplankton and detritus. Krill are especially vital because they serve as a critical food source for many species, including fish, seabirds, and marine mammals such as seals and whales. Amphipods are small, shrimp-like animals that are also a significant food source for Arctic fish and seabirds. Together, these zooplankton represent a key link between the primary producers (phytoplankton and sea ice algae) and the higher levels of the Arctic food web.

The next level of the food web consists of various species of fish, which serve as important prey for a wide range of Arctic predators. Arctic cod, for example, is one of the most abundant and ecologically significant fish in the region. It feeds primarily on zooplankton, such as copepods and krill, and in turn, is a crucial food source for many larger animals, including seals, seabirds, and whales. Capelin, another small schooling fish, also plays a vital role in the Arctic food web. These fish consume zooplankton and smaller fish, and they are a key prey species for larger predators like cod, seabirds, and marine mammals. In addition to these smaller fish, there are also several species of larger predatory fish in the Arctic, such as Arctic char and halibut. These larger fish feed on smaller fish, crustaceans, and invertebrates, and they are themselves important prey for apex predators in the Arctic, including polar bears, wolves, and larger marine mammals.

Moving further up the food chain, seabirds play a significant role in the Arctic ecosystem. Species like puffins, guillemots, and kittiwakes feed on fish, crustaceans, and other marine life. Seabirds are highly adapted to life in the Arctic, with thick layers of insulating feathers and the ability to dive into the frigid waters in search of prey. Some species, such as the Arctic tern, undertake incredible migrations between the Arctic and the Antarctic each year, covering tens of thousands of miles. These birds rely heavily on the abundance of marine life during the Arctic summer to build up energy reserves for their long journeys. In turn, seabirds are preyed upon by larger predators, such as Arctic foxes and polar bears, particularly when they come ashore to nest. Seabird eggs and chicks provide an important source of food for terrestrial predators during the summer months.

Marine mammals are among the most iconic inhabitants of the Arctic, and they play a pivotal role in the food web. Seals, including ringed seals, bearded seals, and harp seals, are key components of the Arctic ecosystem. They feed primarily on fish and invertebrates, such as Arctic cod and krill, and in turn, are a major food source for polar bears and other predators. Seals are highly adapted to life in the icy waters of the Arctic, with thick layers of blubber to insulate them from the cold and the ability to dive deep beneath the ice to hunt for prey. Ringed seals, in particular, are a critical species in the Arctic food web because they are the primary prey for polar bears, the top predator in the region. Bearded seals, with their long whiskers, are bottom-feeders that hunt for benthic invertebrates like clams and worms, further illustrating the diversity of feeding strategies in the Arctic food web.

Whales are another important group of marine mammals that play a significant role in the Arctic food web. Species such as bowhead whales, beluga whales, and narwhals are iconic Arctic residents. Bowhead whales are filter feeders, consuming vast amounts of zooplankton, such as krill and copepods, by filtering seawater through their baleen plates. This allows them to feed efficiently in the nutrient-rich Arctic waters during the summer months. Bowheads are known for their longevity, with some individuals living for over 200 years, making them one of the longest-living mammals on Earth. Beluga whales, with their distinctive white coloration, are toothed whales that feed on fish, squid, and crustaceans. Narwhals, often called the "unicorns of the sea" due to their long, spiral tusks, also feed on fish and squid. These whale species are themselves preyed upon by killer whales (orcas), which are among the few predators capable of hunting large marine mammals in the Arctic.

At the very top of the Arctic food web are apex predators like polar bears, wolves, and killer whales. Polar bears are perhaps the most well-known Arctic predator, and they are uniquely adapted to life in this harsh environment. They rely heavily on sea ice to hunt their primary prey, seals. Polar bears have a highly specialized hunting strategy, using their incredible sense of smell to locate seals resting on the ice or in breathing holes. Once a seal is located, the bear will patiently wait for hours, or even days, for the right moment to strike. Polar bears are also opportunistic feeders and will scavenge on carcasses, hunt young walruses, or even feed on bird eggs when seals are scarce. As apex predators, polar bears play a crucial role in regulating the populations of their prey species, helping to maintain balance within the Arctic ecosystem.

Killer whales, or orcas, are another top predator in the Arctic food web. These highly intelligent and social animals are known for their cooperative hunting strategies, which allow them to take down large prey such as seals, whales, and even sharks. Orcas have a diverse diet, and their hunting techniques vary depending on the region and the specific prey they are targeting. In the Arctic, orcas are known to hunt seals and other marine mammals, and their presence can have a significant impact on the behavior and distribution of these species.

For example, seals and narwhals may alter their movement patterns to avoid areas where orcas are present, which can influence the overall structure of the food web.

Terrestrial predators, such as Arctic foxes and wolves, also play a vital role in the Arctic food web. Arctic foxes are highly opportunistic and adaptable animals, feeding on a wide variety of prey, including lemmings, birds, and carrion. During the summer months, Arctic foxes often follow polar bears, scavenging on the remains of their kills. In the winter, when food is scarcer, Arctic foxes rely on their excellent hearing to locate small mammals beneath the snow, such as lemmings. Wolves, on the other hand, typically hunt larger prey, such as caribou, muskoxen, and hares. They play a key role in controlling the populations of herbivores in the Arctic tundra, helping to prevent overgrazing and maintaining the balance of the ecosystem.

Herbivores in the Arctic, such as caribou, muskoxen, and lemmings, are essential components of the food web, serving as prey for a variety of predators. Caribou, also known as reindeer, are migratory animals that travel vast distances in search of food. During the summer, they feed on grasses, sedges, and shrubs, while in the winter, they rely on lichens and mosses to survive. Muskoxen are large, woolly herbivores that graze on Arctic vegetation, such as grasses and sedges. They are well-adapted to the cold, with thick coats that protect them from freezing temperatures. Lemmings, small rodents that live in the tundra, play a crucial role in the food web by providing a primary food source for predators such as Arctic foxes, wolves, and birds of prey. The population cycles of lemmings can have a significant impact on the overall structure of the food web, as the abundance or scarcity of these small mammals affects the availability of food for their predators.

The Arctic food web is not just confined to land and sea but also extends to the skies. Birds of prey, such as snowy owls and gyrfalcons, hunt small mammals and birds in the Arctic. Snowy owls, with their striking white plumage, are expert hunters of lemmings, and their populations often fluctuate in response to the abundance of these rodents. Gyrfalcons, the largest of the falcons, are skilled hunters of birds and small mammals, and they play a key role in controlling the populations of these species.

At the bottom of the food web are decomposers, such as bacteria, fungi, and scavengers, which break down dead organic matter and recycle nutrients back into the ecosystem. In the Arctic, decomposers play a vital role in nutrient cycling, as the cold temperatures slow down the rate of decomposition. Scavengers, such as Arctic foxes, ravens, and gulls, also play an important role in cleaning up carcasses and ensuring that no energy is wasted in the food web.

In conclusion, the Arctic food web is a finely tuned system of interactions between producers, consumers, and decomposers. Every organism, from the smallest plankton to the largest predators, plays a vital role in maintaining the balance of this fragile ecosystem. The extreme conditions of the Arctic, including the long, dark winters and the brief, intense summers, create a unique set of challenges for the species that call this region home. However, despite these challenges, the Arctic food web has evolved to be incredibly resilient, with species that are highly adapted to the cold and unpredictable environment. However, the ongoing threat of climate change is putting increasing pressure on the Arctic food web. The melting of sea ice, warming temperatures, and changing weather patterns are disrupting the delicate balance of life in the Arctic, with far-reaching consequences for the entire ecosystem. As the Arctic continues to warm at an unprecedented rate, the future of the species that depend on this ecosystem is uncertain. The Arctic food web is a powerful reminder of the interconnectedness of all life on Earth, and the urgent need to protect and preserve this unique and vulnerable environment for future generations.

Chapter 19: Icebreaker Ships and Their Importance

Icebreaker ships play a crucial role in navigating the frozen waters of the Arctic and Antarctic, allowing for essential maritime operations, scientific research, and access to remote regions that would otherwise be inaccessible for much of the year. These specialized vessels are designed to break through thick sea ice, creating navigable channels for other ships, transporting goods, conducting scientific expeditions, and even supporting military operations. The importance of icebreaker ships extends beyond their practical function as they are a symbol of human ingenuity and our ability to adapt to and explore some of the planet's most hostile environments.

The design and construction of icebreaker ships are highly specialized, making them distinct from ordinary ships. Their hulls are heavily reinforced with thick steel to withstand the immense pressure exerted by the ice. Unlike regular ships that have sharp bows to cut through water, icebreakers have sloping bows that are designed to ride up onto the ice and then use the ship's weight to break it. This feature allows them to break through ice that can be several meters thick. Icebreaker ships are also equipped with extremely powerful engines that provide the necessary force to push through dense ice fields. Some of the most advanced icebreakers use nuclear power to generate the massive amounts of energy required to traverse the thickest ice. This design enables icebreakers to clear paths through frozen waters, allowing other vessels—whether they are cargo ships, scientific research ships, or even cruise liners—to follow behind them safely.

One of the most critical roles of icebreaker ships is ensuring that essential supply routes remain open in the Arctic and Antarctic regions. During the winter months, when the ice is at its thickest, many of the northernmost regions, including parts of Canada, Alaska, Russia, and

Greenland, are cut off from the rest of the world. Communities living in these remote areas rely on regular deliveries of food, fuel, and other essential goods. Icebreakers are essential in keeping these shipping lanes open, ensuring that these communities can access vital supplies. For example, icebreakers operating in the Russian Arctic help keep the Northern Sea Route open during the winter, providing a crucial link between Europe and Asia. This route, which runs along Russia's northern coast, significantly shortens the shipping distance between the Atlantic and Pacific oceans compared to traditional routes through the Suez or Panama canals. Without icebreakers, the Northern Sea Route would be impassable for much of the year due to thick ice, cutting off this critical shipping lane and the economic opportunities it provides.

Icebreakers are also indispensable for scientific research in the polar regions. The Arctic and Antarctic are two of the least explored and most scientifically important regions on Earth. They are home to unique ecosystems, critical climate systems, and vast reserves of natural resources. However, the extreme environmental conditions make these areas incredibly difficult to access. Icebreaker ships enable scientists to reach remote areas of the polar ice caps to conduct vital research on topics such as climate change, oceanography, and glaciology. These ships serve as floating research platforms, equipped with laboratories and equipment that allow scientists to collect data on the atmosphere, oceans, ice sheets, and marine life. For example, icebreakers are used to study the effects of melting sea ice on global ocean currents, which play a critical role in regulating Earth's climate. Icebreakers are also used in ecological studies to monitor the health of Arctic and Antarctic ecosystems, which are among the most vulnerable to climate change. The data collected from these expeditions are crucial for understanding how the polar regions are changing and for predicting the future impacts of global warming on the rest of the planet.

The role of icebreakers in supporting military operations in the polar regions is another important aspect of their significance. As interest in the Arctic grows, particularly due to the potential for resource extraction and new shipping routes, countries with Arctic coastlines, such as Russia, the United States, and Canada, are increasing their military presence in the region. Icebreakers play a key role in these efforts by providing year-round access to the Arctic for naval vessels and other military assets. For example, the United States operates icebreakers as part of its Coast Guard fleet, ensuring that it can maintain a presence in the Arctic and protect its national interests. Russia, which has the largest fleet of icebreakers in the world, uses these ships to support its extensive Arctic infrastructure, including military bases, research stations, and energy exploration activities. Icebreakers are also used to patrol and monitor shipping lanes, ensuring that they remain safe and navigable, and to enforce territorial claims in disputed areas of the Arctic. As geopolitical competition in the Arctic heats up, the importance of icebreakers in securing access to this strategically important region will continue to grow.

In addition to their practical applications, icebreaker ships are essential for search and rescue missions in the polar regions. The Arctic and Antarctic are notoriously dangerous places for ships to operate due to the extreme cold, unpredictable weather, and treacherous ice conditions. In the event of an emergency, such as a ship becoming trapped in the ice or suffering a mechanical failure, icebreakers are often the only vessels capable of reaching the stranded ship to provide assistance. These ships are equipped with the technology and personnel needed to conduct search and rescue missions in some of the most challenging environments on Earth. The ability of icebreakers to reach remote areas quickly and break through thick ice can be the difference between life and death for those involved in an emergency situation. As shipping traffic in the Arctic increases due to melting ice and the opening of new routes, the need for icebreaker-assisted search and rescue operations is likely to grow.

One of the most significant challenges facing icebreaker ships today is the growing impact of climate change. As global temperatures rise, the polar ice caps are melting at an alarming rate, leading to profound changes in the Arctic and Antarctic environments. While this may seem to reduce the need for icebreakers, as less ice could mean more accessible waters, the reality is more complex. The melting of the polar ice is leading to the formation of thinner but more unpredictable and dynamic ice conditions. In many areas, the ice is breaking up and refreezing in new patterns, creating dangerous ice floes that are harder to navigate than the thick, stable ice packs of the past. These new conditions pose significant challenges for ships operating in the Arctic, and icebreakers are increasingly needed to help navigate through these treacherous waters. Moreover, as the Arctic Ocean becomes more accessible due to melting ice, shipping traffic in the region is expected to increase dramatically, leading to a greater demand for icebreakers to ensure safe passage for commercial vessels.

The economic importance of icebreaker ships is also growing as the polar regions become more accessible for resource extraction. The Arctic is believed to hold vast reserves of oil, natural gas, and minerals, making it a highly attractive area for exploration and development. However, accessing these resources is incredibly challenging due to the harsh environmental conditions and the presence of sea ice. Icebreakers are essential for supporting energy exploration and extraction operations in the Arctic by providing access to offshore oil and gas fields, ensuring the safe transport of equipment and personnel, and keeping supply routes open during the winter months. For example, icebreakers are used to escort oil tankers and other ships through ice-covered waters to and from drilling platforms. As the global demand for energy continues to grow, the importance of icebreakers in supporting Arctic resource extraction is likely to increase, making them a key asset for countries and companies involved in these industries.

In recent years, there has been growing international cooperation on the use of icebreaker ships, particularly in the context of scientific research and environmental protection. Several countries, including the United States, Russia, Canada, and Norway, have partnered on joint icebreaker missions to study the polar regions and address the challenges posed by climate change. These collaborative efforts have led to significant advancements in our understanding of the Arctic and Antarctic environments and have helped to promote international cooperation on issues such as environmental conservation and sustainable development. The use of icebreaker ships for these purposes highlights their importance not only as practical tools but also as instruments of diplomacy and collaboration in the face of shared global challenges.

Despite their many advantages, there are also several challenges associated with the operation of icebreaker ships. Building and maintaining icebreakers is an expensive and complex process. These vessels require highly specialized materials and technology to withstand the extreme conditions of the polar regions, and they are typically much more costly to construct than regular ships. The operational costs of icebreakers are also high due to the fuel required to power their massive engines and the need for highly trained crews to operate them safely. Additionally, the environmental impact of icebreakers is a growing concern, particularly as their use increases in the Arctic. The noise and vibrations generated by icebreaking operations can disrupt marine life, particularly marine mammals such as whales and seals, which rely on sound for communication and navigation. The emissions produced by icebreakers, particularly older diesel-powered vessels, also contribute to pollution in the Arctic, further exacerbating the environmental challenges facing the region.

To address some of these challenges, there has been increasing interest in developing more environmentally friendly icebreakers. Some of the most advanced icebreakers in the world, such as Russia's nuclear-powered icebreakers, produce no carbon emissions during operation, making them a cleaner option for Arctic navigation. There is also ongoing research into alternative propulsion systems, such as liquefied natural gas (LNG) and hybrid-electric power, which could reduce the environmental impact of icebreakers. These innovations are crucial for ensuring that icebreakers can continue to play their vital role in the Arctic and Antarctic while minimizing their impact on the fragile ecosystems of these regions.

In conclusion, icebreaker ships are an indispensable tool for human exploration, scientific research, and economic activity in the polar regions. Their ability to navigate through the thick, frozen waters of the Arctic and Antarctic allows us to access some of the most remote and inhospitable areas of the planet. Icebreakers are essential for maintaining shipping lanes, supporting scientific research, conducting search and rescue missions, and enabling resource extraction in these regions. As climate change continues to transform the polar ice caps, the role of icebreakers is becoming even more important, both for ensuring safe navigation and for understanding the changes taking place in these critical environments. However, the growing use of icebreakers also presents challenges, particularly in terms of their environmental impact and the high cost of their construction and operation. As we look to the future, it is essential to continue developing new technologies and international partnerships to ensure that icebreaker ships can continue to play their vital role in the polar regions while minimizing their impact on the environment and promoting sustainable development.

Chapter 20: The Greenland Ice Sheet

The Greenland Ice Sheet is one of the most significant and fascinating features of the Earth's cryosphere. It is the second-largest ice mass in the world, covering approximately 1.7 million square kilometers, which is about 80% of the surface of Greenland. Only Antarctica's ice sheet surpasses it in size. The Greenland Ice Sheet plays a critical role in the global climate system, influencing sea levels, ocean currents, weather patterns, and even the planet's albedo—the measure of how much sunlight is reflected back into space. Understanding the Greenland Ice Sheet is essential not only for comprehending the dynamics of the Arctic region but also for recognizing its importance in the broader context of global environmental systems, particularly in light of climate change.

The formation of the Greenland Ice Sheet began around 2.5 million years ago during the Pleistocene epoch, as Earth's climate entered an ice age and temperatures dropped significantly. The ice sheet has grown and shrunk over time, depending on the natural cycles of glaciation and interglaciation. During periods of glaciation, vast quantities of snow accumulate, compacting into ice and contributing to the thickening of the sheet. During interglacial periods, warmer temperatures lead to melting and retreat of the ice sheet. The ice on Greenland is incredibly thick, reaching depths of over 3,000 meters in some areas. If the entire Greenland Ice Sheet were to melt, it is estimated that global sea levels would rise by about 7.4 meters (24 feet), a dramatic increase that would have catastrophic effects on coastal regions around the world.

The Greenland Ice Sheet is composed of layers of compressed snow and ice, which contain valuable information about the Earth's climate history. Each layer represents a year of snowfall, and by drilling deep ice cores into the sheet, scientists can study trapped air bubbles and other particles from thousands of years ago. These ice cores provide a detailed record of past atmospheric conditions, including levels of greenhouse gases such as carbon dioxide and methane, as well as information on temperature variations, volcanic eruptions, and other environmental changes. By analyzing these ice cores, scientists can better understand the natural climate variability over millennia and how human activities have influenced the climate in more recent times.

One of the most critical functions of the Greenland Ice Sheet is its role in regulating global sea levels. As temperatures have risen over the past century due to human-induced climate change, the Greenland Ice Sheet has been losing mass at an accelerating rate. This is a result of increased surface melting and the calving of icebergs from the edges of the sheet into the surrounding ocean. The ice sheet is particularly vulnerable to climate change because of a phenomenon known as the ice-albedo feedback loop. As the ice melts, it exposes darker land or ocean surfaces underneath, which absorb more solar radiation than the reflective white ice. This leads to further warming and more melting, creating a self-reinforcing cycle. The melting of the Greenland Ice Sheet is one of the major contributors to the ongoing rise in global sea levels, which threatens to inundate low-lying coastal areas, displace millions of people, and disrupt ecosystems and infrastructure.

In addition to its impact on sea levels, the melting of the Greenland Ice Sheet affects ocean currents, particularly the Atlantic Meridional Overturning Circulation (AMOC), a critical component of the global ocean conveyor belt. The AMOC is responsible for transporting warm water from the tropics northward and returning cold water to the south. As the Greenland Ice Sheet melts, it releases large amounts of fresh water into the North Atlantic Ocean. This influx of fresh water can disrupt the density-driven circulation of ocean currents by diluting the saltwater, making it less dense and less able to sink and drive the circulation. A slowdown or disruption of the AMOC could have far-reaching effects on global climate patterns, potentially leading to more extreme weather events, such as heatwaves and cold spells, and altering precipitation patterns in various regions.

The Greenland Ice Sheet also plays a crucial role in the Arctic climate by influencing local weather patterns and ecosystems. The cold air masses that form over the ice sheet help to regulate temperatures across the Arctic. In addition, the ice sheet affects the hydrology of the region. As ice melts during the warmer months, it contributes to the formation of meltwater streams, rivers, and lakes that flow across Greenland's surface. These freshwater systems are vital for the local ecology, providing habitat for a range of Arctic species, including fish and migratory birds. However, the rapid melting of the ice sheet is changing the hydrological landscape of Greenland, with implications for the ecosystems that depend on these freshwater resources.

Glaciers that flow from the Greenland Ice Sheet are a key part of its dynamics. These glaciers act as outlets for the ice, transporting it from the interior of the sheet to the coast, where it can either melt or break off into the ocean as icebergs. One of the most well-known of these glaciers is the Jakobshavn Glacier on the west coast of Greenland. This glacier is one of the fastest-moving glaciers in the world, and it is a significant contributor to Greenland's ice loss. The speed of glaciers like Jakobshavn has increased in recent years due to the warming of the region, leading to more ice being transported to the ocean and contributing to rising sea levels.

The edges of the Greenland Ice Sheet, particularly its outlet glaciers, are also influenced by interactions with the surrounding ocean. Warmer ocean currents are reaching the base of these glaciers, accelerating their melting from below. This process, known as "basal melting," is a major factor in the destabilization of the ice sheet. As ocean temperatures continue to rise due to climate change, this process is expected to increase, further accelerating the loss of ice from Greenland and its contribution to sea-level rise.

The Greenland Ice Sheet is also home to a unique subglacial hydrological system, which includes a network of lakes, rivers, and channels that lie beneath the ice. These subglacial features are formed by meltwater that collects under the ice and flows toward the ocean. This water can act as a lubricant, reducing friction between the ice and the underlying bedrock, which can cause glaciers to flow more rapidly. Scientists are only beginning to understand the complexities of these subglacial systems, but they are believed to play a significant role in the dynamics of the ice sheet and its response to climate change.

In recent years, satellite technology has revolutionized the way scientists monitor the Greenland Ice Sheet. Satellites equipped with radar and laser altimetry can measure changes in the thickness of the ice sheet with incredible precision. These measurements have revealed that the ice sheet is thinning at an alarming rate, particularly along its edges. Other satellite systems, such as the GRACE (Gravity Recovery and Climate Experiment) mission, measure changes in the Earth's gravitational field to detect variations in the mass of the ice sheet over time. Together, these technologies have provided a comprehensive picture of how the Greenland Ice Sheet is changing and its contributions to global sea-level rise.

The future of the Greenland Ice Sheet is closely tied to the trajectory of global climate change. Under a scenario of continued high greenhouse gas emissions, the ice sheet could lose a significant portion of its mass by the end of the century, with devastating consequences for sea levels. Even under more moderate emissions scenarios, the ice sheet is likely to continue losing mass for decades to come. However, if global efforts to reduce emissions are successful, it may be possible to slow the rate of ice loss and mitigate some of the most severe impacts on sea levels.

Despite the challenges posed by climate change, there is still much we can learn from the Greenland Ice Sheet. Ongoing scientific research is critical for improving our understanding of how the ice sheet will respond to future warming and for developing strategies to manage the impacts of sea-level rise. In recent years, researchers have increasingly focused on the potential for "tipping points" in the ice sheet's behavior. These tipping points refer to thresholds beyond which the loss of ice could become irreversible, leading to a rapid and unstoppable collapse of parts of the ice sheet. Understanding these tipping points is crucial for predicting the future stability of the Greenland Ice Sheet and the risks it poses to global sea levels.

In addition to its scientific importance, the Greenland Ice Sheet is a key part of Greenland's cultural and economic identity. Greenland's Inuit population has lived in close proximity to the ice sheet for thousands of years, and it has shaped their way of life. The ice sheet provides freshwater, influences local weather patterns, and contributes to the traditional hunting and fishing practices that are central to Inuit culture. However, the rapid changes occurring in the ice sheet due to global warming are having a profound impact on these communities. Hunters and fishermen are finding it increasingly difficult to navigate the changing landscape, and the loss of sea ice is threatening the livelihoods of those who depend on Arctic marine ecosystems.

Tourism is another growing industry in Greenland that is closely tied to the ice sheet. As the Arctic becomes more accessible due to melting ice, there has been an increase in visitors to Greenland who come to witness the breathtaking beauty of its glaciers, icebergs, and rugged landscapes. This influx of tourists has both positive and negative effects. On the one hand, it provides economic opportunities for Greenland's small population. On the other hand, increased human activity in sensitive areas can exacerbate environmental degradation and strain local resources.

In conclusion, the Greenland Ice Sheet is an extraordinary and dynamic component of the Earth's cryosphere, with far-reaching implications for global sea levels, climate systems, and ecosystems. Its massive scale and ancient history make it a critical area of study for scientists seeking to understand past and present climate conditions. However, the Greenland Ice Sheet is also at the forefront of the climate change crisis, as its accelerated melting threatens to reshape coastlines and ecosystems around the world. Protecting and studying this vital ice sheet is essential for mitigating the impacts of climate change and ensuring a sustainable future for the planet. As we continue to learn more about the Greenland Ice Sheet, it serves as a powerful reminder of the fragility of Earth's polar regions and the urgent need for global action to address climate change.

Epilogue

As our journey through the Arctic Circle comes to an end, we've explored a world like no other. We've seen the powerful forces of nature, from the dazzling Northern Lights to the massive glaciers that shape the land. We've met the incredible animals that call this frozen realm home, and we've learned about the people who have adapted to life in one of the harshest environments on Earth.

The Arctic is a place of wonder and beauty, but it is also fragile. The changing climate is affecting everything we've discovered in these pages, from the habitats of polar bears to the traditions of the Inuit people. It's a reminder that this unique part of our world needs our care and respect.

But just as the Arctic has inspired explorers and adventurers for centuries, it can also inspire us to take action. Whether it's learning more about the environment, supporting conservation efforts, or simply sharing what you've learned with others, every little bit helps to protect this incredible region.

As you close this book, remember that the Arctic Circle is not just a distant, icy place on a map—it's a vital part of our planet. And who knows? Maybe one day, you'll find yourself standing on the snowy tundra, looking up at the shimmering auroras, and feeling the magic of the Arctic Circle for yourself.

The End.